INTRODUCTION TO COMPUTER APPLICATION

VIJAY KUMAR PANDEY

Made with ♥ on the Notion Press Platform
www.notionpress.com

This book is dedicated to my wife jaya and son vishwesh pandey. i know without their support it is not possible to complete this.

Contents

Foreword

One day in the afternoon suddenly I got a call from a publisher. He requested me to write a book for Fundamentals of Computer for B.Com course. Those days the Corona period was going on, I was also not very busy, so I agreed. This was my first experience writing a completely new book. The publisher told me that now there is no book on this subject in the market, so you should write as soon as possible. This book was completed in about 3 months and I handed it over to him but even after 2 years the publisher did not publish my book. Recently I came to know about online publishing. and this book is in front of you

The main aim of this book is to provide the basic fundamental details of computer for the MGKVP B.com student. Book is based on New Education Policy 2020.but anyone who want to know some basic fact about computer ststenm cab read thid book.

Preface

The purpose of writing this book is to provide the readers with various aspects of fundamental knowledge of computers, DBMS, database language and word processing. This book is structured to cover key aspects of computer fundamentals.

To a great extent, care has been taken that even if the reader does not have any basic computer knowledge, he can easily understand all the topics.

This book, introduction to computer applications, has been written in conformity with the syllabus for B.com first year as per the common minimum syllabus designed for Uttar Pradesh universities. The book has been divided into 11 chapters.

The very first chapter builds the foundation for understanding various concepts of computer systems. It mainly covers all the necessary topics that are required to give a better start to studying computer systems. The second chapter describes the number system and codes which are essential for developing a better understanding of computers. It requires a little mathematical knowledge. General-purpose software packages are discussed in the third chapter while the fourth, fifth, and sixth chapters deal with various important topics related to a database management system. The seventh chapter introduces the programming language, although it is a broad subject of computer science, here some information is being given so that the reader can clearly understand the working of the software. The eighth chapter discusses data processing from different perspectives. The ninth chapter deals with the conceptual approach to data and file organization; it also describes how computers save our data. The word processor, a unit of PC software package, is explained in detail in the tenth chapter. How to use a word processor has been taught in the 11th chapter. Although many word processors are in use, Microsoft Word is very popular word processor software, so the steps have been explained in the book keeping MS Word in mind. The last chapter introduces data communication and networking, which is not only essential for the students of a particular subject but is also expected of every conscious and educated individual because data communication and networking is the cornerstone of the Internet, which is indispensable for everyone.

Any suggestions and feedback are welcome for further improvement of the text.

Acknowledgements

Not even a leaf moves without the grace of God. It is the blessings of God that I am able to present this book in front of you.

Writing a book is more difficult than I thought. This would not have been possible without the inspiration from my college colleague Dr. Brijesh Yadav. Along with this Dr. Shailendra Tiwari, Anand Mohan Pandey, Sujit Singh, Ashutosh Srivastava and other senior teachers of the college have also been fully cooperative.

CHAPTER ONE

INTRODUCTION TO COMPUTER SYSTEM

Before going to study the various aspect of computer systems one thing must be understood that the study of computers is essential; not only to complete your academic curriculum but also for easiness of your daily routine life. So if you understand the computer system you can live your life better.

1. COMPUTER : AN INTRODUCTION

Nowadays there are so many electronic devices that are used for any kind of task. Most of them are computers. Computers are used in many different forms like desktop, laptop, mobile phone, microwave oven, smart TV, smart refrigerator, music system, etc.

So the computer is not used in a single manner. For example, if you think about a ceiling fan a particular picture will come to your mind and that is correct because of ceiling fan comes mostly in a single shape of the design. But if you think about computers and only a single picture comes to your mind; it is wrong. The computer comes in a very broad manner sometimes directly like a desktop computer and sometimes indirectly like smart TV.

Definition: we can define a computer in different perspectives like a Computer is a machine, a computer is an electronic device, a Computer is a data processor, and the Computer is a digital device. Etc. but in a much-summarized way...

A computer is a digital device that takes data process it under some specific program and produces some meaningful output.

Mainly computer is a digital data problem solver or action performer. It takes data to process it on the basis of some previously loaded program (set of instructions) and produces the desired result. A computer can't do anything that is not pre-loaded into it.

Like many other machines, a computer is also a system. Any system has three main components input-process-output. As our human body, we listen from our ear process it under our brain and when we find some result we can show the output with the help of mouth (speak) or hand (writing). No system can work independently. Like many other systems, computers are also a system, it takes command, instructions, raw data, etc. with the help of specified input devices and then processes it with a special device that is called processor (processor work on preloaded program) and then produces a result. It can be understood with an example suppose that you want to find the result of 15 * 5 to do this you can take the help of a computer. The computer takes input (15 * 5) then the processor processing it on the basis of a table program that is preloaded and gets the result i.e. 75. But how could you know the result so there are some output devices which are used to show the result that is produced by the processor? In very short we can say that a computer is a system for data processing.

1.2 Characteristics of computer

I. **Speed** The speed of computers is very fast. It can perform in a few seconds the amount of work that human beings can do in an hour. When we are talking about the speed of a computer we do not talk in terms of seconds or even milliseconds it is nanoseconds. The computer can perform about 3 to 4 million arithmetic operations per second. The unit of speed of the computer is Hertz. A normal desktop computer processor speed is between 3.50 to 4.2 GHz.

I. **Accuracy** accuracy of computer is very high or in other word we can say that if program design is very good Computer cannot do any mistake. Basically, the accuracy of the program is depending on the accuracy of program writing. So after a long period of time on program testing and the debugging program becomes more accurate. The accuracy of a particular program becomes more accurate Day by day.

III. **Alertness** Computer is a machine so it does not get tired and hence can work for long time without creating any error or mistake. It means that there is no different to perform one arithmetic operation 10 arithmetic operation or for thousand or millions of arithmetic operations the result will be same because of there is no issue of tiredness like human beings. The computer always works on full alert mode.

IV. **Versatility** Modern era demand versatility by everyone. In cricket, the all-rounder is more on the demand of the player. The same player has also liked if the batsman is also a bowler; he is also a good fielder. In the same way, people want to get more and more work from the same machine. Nowadays we can perform any task with the help of computer. we can type, watch movies, listening songs, internet browsing, downloading files, performing much government-related official job using e-governance and so many other useful tasks can be done using a single machine it is called versatility. A computer is capable of performing almost any task provided that the task can be reduced to a series of logical steps.

V. A computer is a digital device that takes data process it under some specific program and produces some meaningful output.

VI. Mainly computer is a digital data problem solver or action performer. It takes data to process it on the basis of some previously loaded program (set of instructions) and produces the desired result. A computer can't do anything that is not pre-loaded into it.

VII. Like many other machines, a computer is also a system. Any system has three main components input-process-output. As our human body, we listen from our ear process it under our brain and when we find some result we can show the output with the help of mouth (speak) or hand (writing). No system can work independently. Like many other systems, computers are also a system, it takes command, instructions, raw data, etc. with the help of specified input devices and then processes it with a special device that is called processor (processor work on preloaded program) and then produces a result. It can be understood with an example suppose that you want to find the result of 15 * 5 to do this you can take the help of a computer. The computer takes input (15 * 5) then the processor processing it on the basis of a table program that is preloaded and gets the result i.e. 75. But how could you know the result so there are some output devices which are used to show the result that is produced by the processor? In very short we can say that a computer is a system for data processing. Computer has a huge storage capacity. We can store millions of libraries on a single computer. A computer can store any amount of information because of its secondary storage. Every piece of information can be stored as long as desired by the user and can be recalled when required. A byte is a storage unit. Normally 1 TB (TeraByte) hard disk is used in desktop. Later we will discuss these units in detail.

VIII. Artificial Intelligence (AI): Above characteristics belong to some traditional computer systems nowadays modern computers come with AI. It means that it can perform much better than previously loaded programs. An artificial intelligence inbuilt computer can take its own decision. Google search is based on artificial intelligence it produces the result of searching on the basis of a particular user searching experience. This type of computer can change the program it can modify the loaded program

1.3 Elements of a Computer System set up:

There are mainly five elements of a computer system.

(i) Hardware the physical part of the computer system that we can see, touch, and move from one place to another is called hardware. For example mouse, keyboard, optical scanner, monitor, printer, processor, etc.

(ii) Software the part of the computer system that we cannot see but the whole system is based on that part, we call it software. Software is mainly a collection of programs. And the program is a set of instructions to solve any given problem or to perform any particular job. All the work of the computer depends on the program. The computer cannot do anything that is not already written in the program, that is, what the computer can do. Everything is already written in the program. Basically, there are two major classifications of software, namely System Software and Application Software.

System software: software that is for a computer system. A computer system consists of many parts so a different type of software is needed for each part. In other, we can say that system software is for hardware. A user can not directly interact with system software but without it, he cannot access the services of particular software. If said in very simple words, then it can be said that the system software acts as an intermediary between the hardware of the computer and the user who uses that computer.

For example, if we want to use a printer, then without printer software (sometimes it is called printer driver software), we cannot use it. With the help of printer software, the computer performs various functions of the printer. Sometimes it is also called device drivers. ROM -BIOS driver, printer driver, USB drivers, motherboard drivers, VGA drivers are some examples of system software. Sometimes the operating system is also considered as system software.

Application software: Application software is the software that is made for a particular work. It is written for a particular application. It is also called end-user software. End-user means that the user interacts with. A computer user directly interacts with it .every application software is written for a particular work for example word processor software is made for only word processing, paintbrush software is made only for painting type of work, the internet browser is used for browsing the internet, etc.

Ms-office, ms-paint, Tux-paint, notepad, adobe reader, Mozilla Firefox, Google Chrome, calculator are some very common examples of application software.

(iii)Human being the most important element of a computer system is its users.

The user's convenience is seen while designing the interface of any application software. We cannot imagine the computer world without human beings. The computer is made by humans and it is made for humans only. Humans cannot be separated from a computer element. Data analysis, computer programmer, server administrator, and computer operators are some important examples of this.

(iv)Data: data is also a very important element of a computer system. Basically, a computer is a data processor so without data, a computer cannot perform anything. Any raw fact is called data and after processing this data becomes information. Suppose we have to find 799 whether it is an odd or even number, then we will call 799 as data, and the rule with which we will find out whether it is even or odd is called a program. And the result that will come out will be output. So both the result and the program depend on our data, so data is mandatory for computers. The same data can present many types of results; hence the demand for data analysis has also increased nowadays. Text, audio, images, and video are some most common forms of data. With the help of appropriate software word processing, image processing, audio processing, and video processing can be performed to get desired output.

(v)Network setup it is not possible to imagine computers without the internet nowadays. Internet is a network of networks. it means that the internet is dependent on various kinds of networks. Most of the networks are belong to the Telecom network for example BSNL, Airtel,jio, etc. So it is very important for the Internet to have this kind of network.

1.4 Components of a Computer System

There are basically three main components of a computer system. Input unit, Process unit, and Output unit. Our computer system is based on these three main components. If we talk about any element of the computer, then it will be related to any one of these three components. To understand the working of the computer, it is very important to understand how these three components are related, and to understand this; we can take the help of a block diagram.

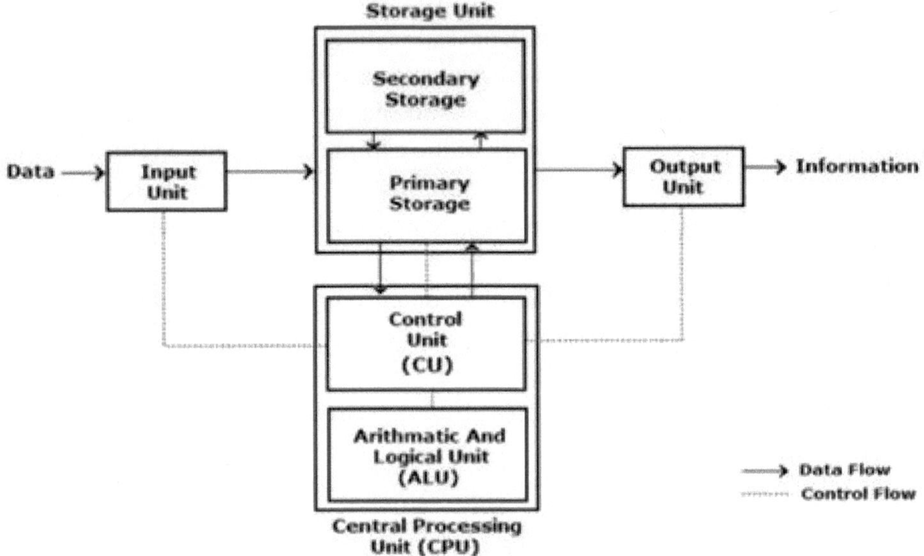

Block Diagram of Computer

Input unit: the main function of this unit is to take data, commands or instructions. To receive data from the user or any other means input devices are used. Mouse, keyboard, joystick, scanner, are some most popular examples of input devices.

Process unit of C.P.U.(central processing unit): this is the core unit of a computer system. It is also called the brain of the computer. Basically, the main task of the computer is done by this unit. Because of this unit computer is called a data processor. In a very simple word, we can say that it is not a part of a computer but it is a computer. The job of this unit is very complicated so it consists of three parts CPU, memory, and storage.

CPU (central processing unit): it is a combination of ALU (arithmetic and Logical unit) and CU (control unit).ALU performs an arithmetic operation such as addition; subtraction etc. and CU perform control operation of the computer system.

Memory: it is a helper of the CPU. As you know we cannot do anything without memory in the same way CPU also needed memory to store temporary data in the meanwhile of processing. It is used from taking data from input devices to show the result. Everywhere temporary memory is required. To do this RAM (Random Access Memory) is used along with the CPU. There is also a special type of memory is used that is call ROM (Read Only Memory).it holds data permanently. It is very costly so only the data that is required for opening the computer is stored in it. So it can be said that there are two types of computer memory RAM and ROM. always remember only RAM is called computer main memory. It is also called primary storage devices.

Storage: there is some difference between storage and memory. In general computer, term memory refers to temporary whereas storage means permanent storage. Mainly secondary storage devices are used for users, not for computers. This means that secondary storage devices are not used in the data processing. The main purposes of these devices are to keep user data or system produced useful information for a long period of time. Examples of these devices are hard disk, CD, DVD, pen drive, memory card, etc. it is cheaper than primary storage ROM. generally, it is used to store a huge amount of data. A normal HDD can store 1/2 terabytes of data.

Output units generally user interact with the input units and output units. After performing very complex data processing job processor produce a result but it is in electronic form human being cannot understand it. So to convert results into human-readable form output devices are used. The main function of the output unit is to convert digital data into a human-understandable form. Monitor and printer are the two most common output devices. Monitor display the result in a soft form on-screen and the printer produce the result on paper in a hard form so sometimes soft copy and hard copy terms are used for monitor and printer respectively. Speaker is also an output device that is used to produce audio for listening.

1.5 Computer Generations

We can divide the generation of computers into five stages. The sequence of computer generation is as follows.

First Generation (1940-1956)

• The period of 1940 to 1956, considered as the First Generation of Computer.

• Vacuum tubes or thermionic valve machines are used in first-generation computers.

• Punched card and the paper tape were used as an input device.

• For output printouts were used.

• ENIAC (Electronic Numerical Integrator and Computer) was the first electronic computer introduced in this generation.

Second Generation (1956-1963)

• The time period from 1956 to 1963 is considered as the second generation of Computers.

• Transistor technologies were used in this generation in place of the vacuum tubes.

• Second-generation computers have become much smaller than the first generation.

• Computation speed of second-generation computers was much faster than the first generation so it takes lesser time to produce results.

Third Generation (1963-1971)

• The time period from 1963 to 1971 is considered the Third Generation of computers.

• Third generation of computers is based on Integrated Circuit (IC) technology.

• Third generation computers became much smaller in size than the first and second generation, and their computation power increased dramatically.

• The third generation computer needs less power and also generated less heat.

• The maintenance cost of the computers in the third generation was also low.

• Commercialization of computers was also started in this generation.

Fourth Generation (1972-2010)

• The time period from 1972 to 2000 is considered as Third Generation of computers.

• The invention of microprocessor technology laid the foundation for the fourth generation computer.

• Fourth generation computers not only became very small in size, but their ability to calculate also increased greatly and at the same time they became portable, that is, it became very easy to move them from one place to another.

• The computers of fourth-generation started generating a very low amount of heat.

• It is much faster and accuracy became more reliable because of microprocessor technology.

• Their prices have also come down considerably.

• Commercialization of computers has become very fast and it is very easily available for common people.

Fifth Generation (2010- till date)

• The time period from 1972 to 2000 is considered as Third Generation of computers.

• AI (Artificial intelligence) is the backbone technology of this generation of computers. AI-enabled computers or programs behave like an intelligent person that's why this technology is called artificial intelligence technology.

• In addition to intelligence, the speed of computers has also increased significantly and the size has also reduced much earlier than even the computer on the palm has been used.

• Some of the other popular advanced technologies of the fifth generation include Quantum computation, Nanotechnology, Parallel processing, Big Data, and IoT, etc.

1.6 computer language

A computer cannot understand our language because it is a machine. So, it understands machine language or we can say that the main language of computers is machine language. Now the question arises that which language a machine understands? The answer is very easy; it understands the language of on and off.

But due to the complexity of the work of computers nowadays, it is not easy to work with the computer only in the language of on and off, so some other languages are used for the computer.

Therefore, the language of computers is mainly divided into three parts.

1. Machine language: - Machine language is the language in which only 0 and 1 two digits are used. Any digital device only understands 0 and 1.It is the primary language of a computer that the computer understands directly, the number system which has only two digits is called a binary number system so we can say that the computer can understand only binary codes. Binary codes have only two digits 0 and 1 since the computer only understands the binary signal i.e. 0 and 1 and the computer's circuit i.e. the circuit recognizes these binary codes and converts it into electrical signals. In this, 0 means Low /off and 1 means High/ On.

2. Assembly Language: - We use symbols in assembly language because machine language is difficult for humans, so assembly language was used to make communication with the computer easier. That is why it is also called symbol language. Sometimes it is also called low-level language. But one thing must be understood that the computer understands only and only the language of the machine. So the computer needs a special type of program, called assembler, to understand the assembly language. The assembler converts programs written in assembly language into machine language so that the program written by us can be understood by the computer. Assembly language is the second generation of programming language.

3. High-Level Language: - Symbols were used in assembly language, so it was difficult to write a program with only symbols, so the need was felt for a language that uses the alphabet of ordinary English or we can say it that we can understand and write easily. Writing and understanding high-level language is much easier than assembly language, so it is quite popular in the computer world with the help of which it became very easy to write many programs. As the assembler was used to convert assembly language to machine language, a special type of software called compiler is used to convert high-level language to machine language. Some of the major high-level programming languages are C, C ++, JAVA, HTML, PASCAL, Ruby, etc.

1.6 Types of Computer

Computers can be broadly classified by their speed and computing power.

- **PC (Personal Computer)** it is a single user computer system having average speed microprocessor. It is a general purpose computer. Common people use this type of computer system.
- **WorkStation** It is also a single-user computer system that is similar to a personal computer but has a more powerful microprocessor.
- **Mini Computer** It is a multi-user computer system that is capable of supporting hundreds of users simultaneously.
- **Main Frame** It is a multi-user computer system that is capable of supporting thousands of users simultaneously. Software technology is different from minicomputers.
- **Supercomputer** It is an extremely fast computer which can perform millions of millions of instructions per second.

1.7 computersinbusiness

Profit maximization is the fundamental goal of any business. Due to the unlimited capabilities of computers, it is used in business. It becomes an essential component of any business. Due to its speed, accuracy, and network, it is preferred in all businesses. Most people nowadays are emphasizing performing automatic operations whether it is banking, telecom, insurance, railway, and other sectors. It has become more convenient to done more and more work by computer. and see if computer The most useful for the business itself is because the main objective is to make maximum use of any component in the business whether it is workers or raw materials or machinery, a successful businessman makes maximum use of them only then his profit will also be maximized. And the computer has all these features because it not only produces results at a fast pace, but it is also less likely to be wrong. We can say that a computer in business is the same as a supremely reliable servant at home. Today, you cannot even think of doing any business without a computer. Computers are very popular in the business sector. Computers are used in purchasing raw materials and transporting them to the consumer, even now the use of computers has started in payment. There is no such element of business where there is no access to computers.

Nowadays, no big or small business can be done without this machine. Areas such as sales and marketing, retailing, banking, stock trading are growing very fast. That is why it is very important for the Employees of every Business Organization to understand the customer and have marketing knowledge as well as knowledge of Computer Technology.

The Internet has a huge contribution for marketing or to spread the business far and wide. And without a computer, the Internet is nothing. Now it is not that time where people carry cash. Everything has changed, Debit cards, internet banking, electronic deposit, bill paying, money is being transacted from the online stock itself. Online shopping has become a store of people. Along with this, their use is very much in some of the works given below.

- For billing.
- Online payment
- For payroll management system
- sales analysis
- Financial forecasting
- Account management
- Record keeping
- Inventory management
- Decision making system with data analysis
- Production management
- Online advertisement
- Social media marketing
- Digitization of complete business data
- Data security
- Business data recovery and backup.

1.7 Indian computing environment

In India, it is a challenge to change the computing environment completely. However, in the last few years, there has been a lot of technological development in India. But it is not sufficient to face the global completion. So if want to compete with the global challenges we must adopt office automation. While on one hand, the basic infrastructure has to be increased in India, on the other hand, people will also have to be proficient in office automation. Office automation does not just mean that we install a computer or use communication devices in the office. It means much more comprehensive, it includes a lot of technologies. Office automation includes many latest technologies to improve the proficiency of the office. If seen, the work of an office can be done manually, but the challenge in front of today's office is not possible for any organization without adopting automation. Today office automation has become an essential component for any organization. Today's office has a lot of needs increasing office efficiency reducing the overhead of administration providing good facilities to the customer, making communication fast and reliable.

The Indian computing environment is basically based on office work. Because of office is a place where many kinds of work have to be performed on a single place. We can say that office provides an integrated environment of several different nature of task like type a document is different from sending messages.

Before computers, all the office work was done by human beings. Therefore, they used to take a lot of time to do some work and they were also more likely to make mistakes. With the advent of computers, there has been a complete change in the functioning of the office. And if seen, the entire map of the office has changed. Manual work is almost done. The functioning of the office is not only dependent on the computer, but it has also moved towards automation, it uses the latest technology to increase the capacity of the overall office.

Following are some general office tasks

- Document preparation, typing and printing.
- Report writing and presentation
- Information processing
- Document distribution
- Mailing letters
- Designing related work
- Data entry
- Account maintenance
- Record keeping
- Communication with internal employee
- Communication with external parties.

Exercises

Objective type question

Choose the correct answer for the followings

1. The brain of any computer system is called

a. ALU b. Memory c. CPU d. Control unit

2. Which part receives program instructions and initiates control operations?

a. Input unit b. Storage unit c. Logic unit d. Control unit

3. Which of the following computer language is not known as High-Level Language?

a. c++ b. java c. HTML d. machine language

4. A computer program that converts assembly language to machine language is known as

a. Compiler b. Interpreter c. Assembler d. Comparator

5. Any type of storage that is used for holding data between steps in its processing is

a. CPU b. Primary storage c. Intermediate storage d. Internal storage

6. Which computer has been designed to be as compact as possible?

a. Mini b. Supercomputer c. Micro computer d. Mainframe

7. In how many generations a computer can be classified?

a. 5 b. 6 c. 4 d. 3

8. Fifth generation computers are based on

a. Artificial intelligence b. programming intelligence c. oops d. VLSIC

9. Any data or instruction entered into the memory of a computer is considered as

a. Storage b. Output c. Input d. Information

10. Microsoft Word is an example of

a. an operating system b. processing device c. application software
d. an input device

Theoretical questions

1. What do you mean by a computer? Explain the basic concept of a computer system.
2. List out and explain some of the important characteristics of a computer.
3. What is meant by generation in computer terminology how many computer generations are there till now?
4. Draw an illustrative block diagram of the computer system and explain the functions of the various units.
5. Describe the role of computers in business.
6. Write a short note on the Indian computing environment.
7. Differentiate between hardware and software.
8. What do you mean by computer languages explain with suitable example?

CHAPTER TWO

NUMBER SYSTEM AND CODES

2.1 Number System

You might be thinking that where did this number system in the computer world come from?

So before we go into the details about the number system, it is important to know why we are reading the number system.

A computer is a digital device. It works with digital signals and a digital signal is based on discrete signal means it has not very spread like an analog signal. Digital signal has only two values either on/off or high/low. So it can be easily represented by two numbers i.e. 1 and 0.

As you know CPU is known as the brain of the computer system. it means that it is very important for computers. Basically, the task of CPU is ultimately done by a device known as a microprocessor. The architecture of microprocessors is very very complicated. So in the form of signal only, it is very difficult to represent various functions of a computer. Number representation makes it easy. That's why we study the number systems.

Some basic number system is as follow:

i) Binary number system:

The binary number system is a very much suitable number system for the computer because it consists of only two numbers 1 and 0. The computer is also based on two signals.

Characteristics of binary number system

Base: 2 (how many numbers are used)

Values: 0 1

ii) Decimal number system:

A standard number system is used universally in arithmetic. The decimal number system is very common in our daily life and you are very much familiar with this.

Characteristics of decimal number system

Base: 10 (how many numbers are used)

Values: 0 1 2 3 4 5 6 7 8 9

iii) Octal number system:

An important number system is used in some computer codes.

Characteristics of octal number system

Base: 8 (how many numbers are used)

Values: 0 1 2 3 4 5 6 7

iv) Hexadecimal number system:

A useful number system for the representation of long character sets.

Characteristics of Hexadecimal number system

Base: 16 (how many numbers are used)

Values: 0 1 2 3 4 5 6 7 8 9 A B C D E F

Note: in hexadecimal number system English characters set A is used for 10, B is for 11, and so on.

2.2 Number System Conversion

Now we will learn to convert the number of one number system to another number system.

We can divide the whole number system conversion into two main modules.

i. Decimal to other number system
ii. Other number system to decimal number system

2.2.1 Decimal to other number system:

To convert from a decimal number system to another number system, we divide the decimal number by the base value of the other number system (in which to change), the quotient that returns is again divided by the base value of the other number system which is the quotient. Again, divide it by the base value of the other number system and write the remainder separately. This process continues until the quotient becomes 0. In the end, we write the remainders which we had written separately in reverse order, this is our converted number.

For example, suppose we have to convert the decimal number 5 to binary number, then the base value of the binary number system is two, so we will divide 5 by 2, and if 5 is to be converted into an octal number system we will divide 5 by 8 because 8 is the base value of octal number system. Similarly, if it is to be converted into hexadecimal, we will divide 5 by 16 and the rest of the process will remain the same.

Now we will understand it step by step with the help of examples.

a. Decimal to binary:

Conversion steps:

1. Divide the number by 2.
2. If the quotient is not 0 again divide it by 2.
3. Take the remainder for the binary digit.
4. Repeat the steps until the quotient is 0.

Example 1: Find the binary equivalent of a decimal number 5.

$(5)_{10} = (\underline{?})_2$

Solution:

Base value of binary is 2

2(divisor) 5 (dividend)

2 2 (quotient) 1(remainder) ↑

2 1 0 ↑

0 1 ↑

$(5)_{10} = (\underline{101})_2$ Answer 101

Example 2 : Find the binary equivalent of a decimal number 28.

$(28)_{10} = (\underline{?})_2$

Solution:

Base value of binary is 2

Divisor Dividend Quotient

2 28

2 14 0↑

2 7 0 ↑

2 3 1 ↑

2 1 1 ↑

0 1 ↑

$(28)_{10}=(11100)_2$ Answer 11100

(b) Decimal to octal

Conversion steps:

1. Divide the number by 8.
2. If the quotient is not 0 again divide it by 8.
3. Take the remainder for the octal digit.
4. Repeat the steps until the quotient is 0.

Example 1: Find the octal equivalent of a decimal number 5.

$\mathbf{(5)_{10} = (\underline{?})_8}$

Solution:

Base value of octal is 8

8(divisor) 5 (dividend)

0 (quotient) 5(remainder) ↑

$(5)_{10}=(\underline{5})_8$ Answer 5

Example 2: Find the octal equivalent of a decimal number 28.

$\mathbf{(28)_{10} = (\underline{?})_8}$

Solution:

base value of octal is 8

8 28

8 3 4 ↑

8 0 3 ↑

$(28)_{10}=(34)_8$ Answer 34

(c) Decimal to hexadecimal

Conversion steps:

1. Divide the number by 16.
2. If the quotient is not 0 again divide it by 16.
3. Take the remainder for the hexadecimal digit.
4. Repeat the steps until the quotient is 0.

Example 1: Find the hexadecimal equivalent of a decimal number 5.

$\mathbf{(5)_{10} = (\underline{?})_{16}}$

Solution:

Base value of hexadecimal is 16

16(divisor) 5 (dividend)

0 (quotient) 5(remainder) ↑

$(5)_{10}= (\underline{5})_{16}$ Answer 5

Example 2: Find the hexadecimal equivalent of a decimal number 28.

$\mathbf{(28)_{10} = (\underline{?})_{16}}$

Solution:

Base value of hexadecimal is 16

16 28

16 1 12 ↑

0 1 ↑

in hexadecimal 12 is represented by c

$(28)_{10}=(1C)_{16}$ Answer 1C

2.2.2 Other number system to decimal:

In this type of conversion multiply each digit of decimal number to a base value of other number systems with power 0 in increasing order. You can understand it with example very easily.

a. Binary to decimal

Conversion steps:

1. Multiply the rightmost digit of the given binary number with the 2^0 and get the value.
2. Go one digit left (if digit exists) and multiply with the 2^1 and get the value and sum with the previous step multiplication value.
3. Go one digit left (if digit exists) and multiply with the 2^2 and get the value and sum with the previous step multiplication value.
4. Continue the sequence until all digits of a given number are finished.

Note: The power starts from 0 to n-1 where n is the total number of digits in the given binary number.

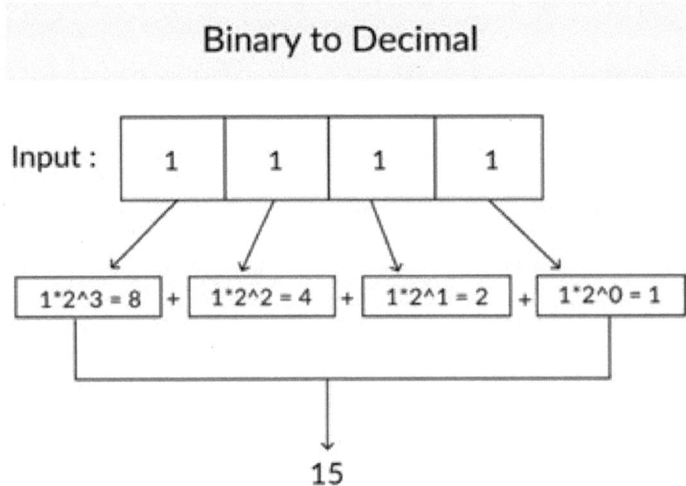

Fig 2.1 Binary to Decimal conversion

Example 1: Find the decimal equivalent of a binary number 101.

$(101)_2 = (\underline{?})_{10}$

Solution:

Base value of binary is 2

Given number: 1 0 1

$1*2^2 + 0+2^1 + 1*2^0$

= 4 + 0 + 1

= 5

$(101)_2$ = (5)$_{10}$ Answer: 5

-à If you again reverse to change 5 into binary you will get 101 from previous method i.e. conversion from decimal to binary.

Example 2: Find the decimal equivalent of a binary number 11100.

$(11100)_2$ = (?)$_{10}$

Solution:

Base value of binary is 2

Given number: 1 1 1 0 0

$1*2^4 + 1+2^3 + 1*2^2 + 0*2^1 + 0*2^0$

= 16 + 8 + 4 + 0 + 0

= 28

$(11100)_2$ = (28)$_{10}$ Answer: 28

(b) Octal to decimal

Conversion steps:

1. Multiply right most digit of the given octal number with the 8^0 and get the value.
2. Go one digit left (if digit exist) and multiply with the 8^1 and get the value and sum with previous step multiplication value.
3. Go one digit left (if digit exist) and multiply with the 8^2 and get the value and sum with previous step multiplication value.
4. Continue the sequence until all digits of given number is finished.

Note: The power starts from 0 to n-1 where n is the total number of digits in the given octal number.

Example 1: Find the decimal equivalent of an octal number 5.

$(5)_8$ = (?)$_{10}$

Solution:

Base value of octal is 8

Given number: 5

$5*8^0$

= 5

$(5)_8$ = (5)$_{10}$ Answer: 5

Example 2: Find the decimal equivalent of an octal number 34.

$(34)_8$ = (?)$_{10}$

Solution:

Base value of octal is 8

Given number: 3 4

$3*8^1 + 4*8^0$

= 24 + 4

= 28

$(34)_8$ = (28)$_{10}$ Answer: 28

(c) Hexadecimal to decimal

Conversion steps:

1. Multiply right most digit of the given hexadecimal number with the 16^0 and get the value.
2. Go one digit left (if digit exist) and multiply with the 16^1 and get the value and sum with previous step multiplication value.
3. Go one digit left (if digit exist) and multiply with the 16^2 and get the value and sum with previous step multiplication value.
4. Continue the sequence until all digits of given number is finished.

Note: The power starts from 0 to n-1 where n is the total number of digits in the given hexadecimal number.

Example 1: Find the decimal equivalent of a hexadecimal number 5.

$(5)_{16} = (\underline{?})_{10}$

Solution:

Base value of hexadecimal is16

Given number: 5

$5*16^0$

= 5*1

=5

$(5)_{16} = (\underline{5})_{10}$ Answer: 5

Example 2: Find the decimal equivalent of a hexadecimal number 1C.

$(1C)_{16} = (\underline{?})_{10}$

Solution:

Base value of hexadecimal is 16

Given number: 1 C

$1*16^1 + c*16^0$

= 16 + 12*1

=16 + 12

= 28

$(1C)_{16} = (\underline{28})_{10}$ Answer: 28

We have seen that how to convert other number systems into decimal and vice versa. So if we have to convert other number systems into other number systems. We can first convert it into decimal and then do the learned process. For example, if we have to convert the octal number into a hexadecimal number, we convert the octal number into a decimal number and then convert it into the hexadecimal number. It can also be applied vice versa.

2.3 Computer codes:

As we have already discussed that binary number system is very suitable for computers. But we have just seen the numerical part of the binary number system. A different approach is used to represent data in computer memory because the numeric value is not complete data.

There are many other things in the data. Character set like a b c d...etc., symbols @ # $ ....etc. space or blank is also a part of data. However, any data must be represented in the computer by the bits 0 & 1. This means the ultimately binary system is used in computer memory but in a different manner.

A method is needed to represent every type of data in a systematic way. For this, a group of n bits is created so that we can display all types of data in n bits. Generally, 8 bits are used to form a group. This group is known as a byte.

However, the term byte is commonly used to mean an 8 bit is equal to a byte because modern computers use 8 bits to represent a symbol.

Some popular digital data storage units are as follow

Unit Short form Equals

Bit b 1 or 0 (on or off)

Byte B 8 bits

Kilobyte KB 1024 bytes

Megabyte MB 1024 kilobytes
Gigabyte GB 1024 megabytes
Terabyte TB 1024 gigabytes
Petabyte PB 1024 terabytes
Exabyte EB 1024 petabytes
Zettabyte ZB 1024 exabytes
Yottabyte YB 1024 zettabytes

Bits are the basic units of data storage. Computers use binary digits, a long series of 0's and 1's. These binary digits are known as bits, it is the smallest possible unit for data storage.

When 8 bits are combined in a group, we get a byte. Basically, bytes are used to store a single character data; the weather's it is an alphabet, number, any symbols, or punctuation. All memory storage is represented in terms of bytes, so if bits are the foundation of data storage, bytes are the building blocks of data storage.

BCD and ASCII are two commonly used computer codes.

2.3.1 Binary-coded decimal (BCD)

Binary-coded decimal (BCD) is a binary encoding scheme of decimal numbers and alphabets where each digit is represented by a predefined standard number of bits, usually six in a computer. It can represent 64 (26) different characters.

Any individual digit of data can be converted on the basis of the following BCD chart.

BCD chart

Char	BCD Code		Octal
	Zone	Digit	
A	11	0001	61
B	11	0010	62
C	11	0011	63
D	11	0100	64
E	11	0101	65
F	11	0110	66
G	11	0111	67
H	11	1000	70
I	11	1001	71
J	10	0001	41
K	10	0010	42
L	10	0011	43
M	10	0100	44

Char	BCD Code		Octal
	Zone	Digit	
N	10	0101	45
O	10	0110	46
P	10	0111	47
Q	10	1000	50
R	10	1001	51
S	01	0010	22
T	01	0011	23
U	01	0100	24
V	01	0101	25
W	01	0110	26
X	01	0111	27
Y	01	1000	30
Z	01	1001	31

BCD chart

Character	BCD Code		Octal Equivalent
	Zone	Digit	
1	00	0001	01
2	00	0010	02
3	00	0011	03
4	00	0100	04
5	00	0101	05
6	00	0110	06
7	00	0111	07
8	00	1000	10
9	00	1001	11
0	00	1010	12

BCD chart for Numbers

Example 1: Convert BCD equivalent of the word CAT

Solution: On the basis of above mention chart we find that

C = 110011

A = 110001

T = 010011

So the binary digits

110011 110001 010011 is equivalent to English word cat. Means if any computer uses BCD system to store data then the word 'cat' will be store as 110011 110001 010011.

Example 2: Convert a number 28 in BCD representation

Solution: On the basis of BCD chart we can find that

2 = 000010

8 = 001000

So the answer is 000010 001000

2.3.2 ASCII (American standard code for information interchange)

American standard code for information interchange (ASCII) is also a very popular and mostly everywhere used encoding standard. It is of two types ASCII-7 and ASCII-8.ASCII-7 uses 7 bits to represent data and it can represent up to 128 different characters. ASCII-8 uses 8 bits to represent any data and it can represent up to 256 different characters. Like BCD it is also based on an ASCII chart where each digit ASCII value is predefined.

ASCII CHART

Character	ASCII-7 / ASCII-8		Hexadecimal Equivalent
	Zone	Digit	
0	0011	0000	30
1	0011	0001	31
2	0011	0010	32
3	0011	0011	33
4	0011	0100	34
5	0011	0101	35
6	0011	0110	36
7	0011	0111	37
8	0011	1000	38
9	0011	1001	39

ASCII chart

Character	ASCII-7 / ASCII-8		Hexadecimal Equivalent
	Zone	Digit	
A	0100	0001	41
B	0100	0010	42
C	0100	0011	43
D	0100	0100	44
E	0100	0101	45
F	0100	0110	46
G	0100	0111	47
H	0100	1000	48
I	0100	1001	49
J	0100	1010	4A
K	0100	1011	4B
L	0100	1100	4C
M	0100	1101	4D

Character	ASCII-7 / ASCII-8		Hexadecimal Equivalent
	Zone	Digit	
N	0100	1110	4E
O	0100	1111	4F
P	0101	0000	50
Q	0101	0001	51
R	0101	0010	52
S	0101	0011	53
T	0101	0100	54
U	0101	0101	55
V	0101	0110	56
W	0101	0111	57
X	0101	1000	58
Y	0101	1001	59
Z	0101	1010	5A

ASCII CHARTS

Example: convert the English word 'CAT' into ASCII coding scheme.
Solution: on the above mention ASCII chart we can find the equivalence of
C = 0100 0011
A = 0100 0001
T = 0101 0100
So the answer is 01000011 01000001 01010100
Exercises
Objective type question
Choose the correct answer for the followings
1. Which of the following is not a binary number?
(a) 101 (b) 000010 (c) 546 (d) 1C
2. How do you write 5 in binary systems?
(a) 101 (b) 010 (c) 001 (d) 100
3. How do you write 15 in binary system?

(a) 1011 (b) 1111 (c) 0011 (d) 1100
4. What is the base of octal number system?
(a) 2 (b) 4 (c) 8 (d) 16
5. What is the base of hexadecimal number system?
(a) 2 (b) 4 (c) 8 (d) 16
6. The decimal value of binary number 100011 is
(a) 3 (b) 25 (c) 22 (d) 35
7. 1 Tb is equal to
(a) 1024 GB (b) 1024Mb (c) 1024kb (d) 10241024 bytes
8. 5 Mb is equal to
(a) 5*1024 byte (b) 1024/5 Kb (c)5*1024 Kb (d) 1024 byte
9. Which of the following is the correct representation of a binary number?
(a) $(124)^2$ b) 1110 c) $(110)_2$ d) $(000)^2$
10. $(35)_8 = (?)_{16}$
(a) $(12)_{16}$ b) (1D) 16 c) $(124)_{16}$ d) $(AC)_{16}$
Theoretical questions
1. What are the 4 types of number systems? Explain with a suitable example.
2. What is the base value of the decimal, hexadecimal, binary, and octal number system?
3. Find out the decimal equivalent of the following binary numbers
(a) 1101011 (b) 11010101 (c) 10011 (d) 11111001 (e)111001 (f)100 (g)101000 (h)1100
4. Find out the binary equivalent of the following decimal number
(a) 5 (b) 55 (c) 125 (d) 300 (e) 526 (f) 100 (g) 10000 (h) 0
5. Define the term byte. What is the difference between a byte and a bit?
6. Write the 6 bit BCD code for the following data
(a) 25 (b) 63 (c) 155 (d) DOG
7. Show the ASCII coding for the following data
(a) 25 (b) 63 (c) 155 (d) DOG
8. What do you mean by computer codes? Explain its importance in storage management.
9. Differentiate between BCD and ASCII.

CHAPTER THREE

PC SOFTWARE PACKAGE

3.1 PC SOFTWARE PACKAGE- An introduction

PC means personal computer.

This is the default computer system. This means we usually understand the same meaning of computer unless stated separately. This is the computer which is commonly used in offices, homes, banks, railways, etc. it is also known as desktop/laptop computer.

As its name suggests, it is for personal use. Used as a personal tool for one person. Computers are also of different types according to different tasks. Software is an essential part of any computer system. In this chapter, we will learn about various important software that are required for any normal personal computer.

For a common man, a computer means only the software used in it. For example, MS Word is the main software for typists. The game's software for the game player .it is similar for different banks, railways, and other people according to their respective subjects. For a normal user computer, a computer simply means software that does its job. It realizes the importance of software. The software has the same place in the computer as the memory of the human being in his mind. For example, suppose you ask for a table of 2, you have an ear and can hear it, but if the same ear does not understand the meaning of 2, then it will not be able to tell the answer. Even then you cannot hear the table. So the table you remember is the software. The more you know things, the higher your importance is. The higher your value is. The more the software is on the computer, the more useful it is for us. But there are countless things in the world, how much do we learn? So, brother, we should learn at least as much as a normal person should, and how much software should be on the computer? How much life is expected to be in a normal computer?

It is therefore quite clear that software is an essential element of any computer system.

There are mainly two types of software, Application software and system software. Application software contains programs that allow us to perform specific tasks for users, such as word processing programs, e-mail programs, or web browsers, etc. System software consists of programs that control the operation of the computer and its various devices. There are two types of system software, operating systems and utility programs. An operating system (OS) is a set of programs that contain instructions that coordinate all activities between computer hardware devices. A utility program performs a specific function, usually related to the management of a computer, its equipment, or its programs.

So in the PC software package, we mainly include software that can be functioned normally. Most important is an operating system, word processor, spreadsheet application, and web browser for the internet. However, the web browser is inbuilt with the operating system itself. It is also a great component of the PC software package. In today's operating system, many application software that is necessary for us are inbuilt such as text editor software that we can just write, they do not have much capacity compared to the word processor. But it is also very important. So notepad, paintbrush for doing minor painting work, photo viewer for viewing photos, calculator for calculating, etc. are some of the essential applications that are installed with the operating system. Therefore, we do not discuss them separately or it is inbuilt with the operating system itself. Word processors have all the necessary elements to work in any office and in a spreadsheet application, there are many tools available for doing work related to calculus an office, we can say that without spreadsheet application in an office It is not possible to do the work, we can say that with the help of word processor and spreadsheet, all the tasks of an office can be done. Even in some companies, the work of an entire office can be conducted with the help of MS Word and Excel.

So finally we can say a software package contains the following for any pc:

i. Operating system
ii. Word processor
iii. Spreadsheet
iv. Browser

(i) Operating system

- An operating system is the most compulsory software of any PC software package.
- An operating system is software that is used to manage different hardware and software resources of a computer system.
- An operating system is a resource manager.
- An operating system is also a mediator between user and computer. It provides us an interface to use many hardware and software components of a computer system.
- An operating system provides an integrated platform for users, different hardware, and system and application software components. Each and every component of a computer system is connected with an operating system.
- An operating system is a tool. With the help of this tool, we can access the computer very easily.
- We cannot do anything without an operating system on a computer. Everything is done on a computer with the help of the operating system.

As we know that the computer is a very complex machine and its components are also very complex. Since the operating system provides an easy interface, with the help of which we can use such a complex machine very easily.

For example, if we have to take air from the fan, the fan has to be installed, we will also have to install a switchboard and regulator in the installation, which does not give us air, but without them, we cannot use the fan properly. The regulator and switchboard of the fan operate in an operating system manner. We provide this interface with the help of which we can use the facility of the fan. In the same way, a computer also has an operating system. Windows is an important and very popular operating system of a desktop computer, with the help of this, we can access very complex parts of the computer such as processor, memory, monitor printers, etc. very easily.

Suppose we have to save a file, the ultimate goal for saving a file is to access a hard disk because a hard disk device is responsible for storing our data permanently. But user cannot access it directly. It is very easy to save files with the help file of the operating system.

Saving, printing, cut copy paste, transferring file or folder from one location to another and device detection are some common task that has to be done by the operating system.

After all these things, we can understand why an operating system is necessary for a PC software package. Basically, if you want to learn computer ultimately you have to learn operating system.

Finally, we can say that we cannot imagine a computer system without an operating system .hardware is important, the software is important, but the operating system is most important.

The names of some popular operating systems are as follows.

Windows, Linux, UNIX, android (mobile Smartphone), mac os, ios.

There are so many operating systems used in the market but Microsoft Windows is the most popular and user-friendly operating system for desktop or laptop computers and Android, the most commonly used operating system in mobile phones

Along with the interfaces, all the modern operating systems that come today, some very common application software are given together. Remember, when we install it, all the application software is installed along with the operating system itself. There is no need to install them separately

---- Text editor or notepad

It is used for writing plain text or writing a normal letter. It has very limited features like cut copy paste, font size selection, find a text, etc.

Supporting files of many operating systems are in the form of a notepad itself.

The extension of the Notepad file is .txt

---- Calculator.

It is an application for performing some calculating tasks. An arithmetic calculation can be performed by this application program very easily.

---- Paintbrush.

It is a very popular and useful application found in Microsoft Windows.

With the help of this application drawing and painting can be done on a computer in a very entreating way. Using a Paintbrush we can draw many shapes, design a pattern. Working in a paintbrush looks like working in real. We can use a mouse-like pen pencil or brush and screen-like paper. It is a very common application used for painting using a computer but has not had very advanced features. It is a general-purpose painting application inbuilt with the windows operating system.

---- Game.

Windows and many other operating systems also provide gaming applications.

---- Sound recording

Most of the modern operating system provides sound editing application. In which users can record their audio and edit it very easily. So to perform sound-related tasks user needs not install any other software.

---- Media player

This application is used for playing video and audio files. Some other applications are also used for playing video and audio files such as VLC media player, real take but window media player is the default media player for Windows operating system. Using windows media player we can play many video and audio file such as .mpeg, .mp4, .mkv, .mp3, .dat.

In addition to the above, there are so many other functions that seem to be frequently used, such as copying a file or folder from one location to another or transferring selected files from one location to another on the hard disk. Transfer data to pen drive, connect any other device to computer for anyone. Apart from these, some troubleshooting tasks are also performed by the operating system. Like if the user suddenly shut down the computer. If any data is deleted by mistake, then bring it back.

(ii) Word processor

A computer is a data processor which can process on data. Any kind of data can be processed through a computer. Data may be in the form of text, word, audio, image as well as in video format.

The computer takes the help of many types of applications to do this kind of work; one of them is a word processor.

Word processor is application software used to process the word.

It means that the word processor takes words as input, processes them under the previously loaded program, and produces output words. These output words are the words the user wishes.

The word processor mainly facilitates the formatting of our words. Now we can write the word better with our own flexibility.

Following are some special features of any word processor

> We can convert words into many other different languages and different formats.

> We can create standard documents with the help of an inbuilt template. These templates help a lot to follow the standardization of any specific documents.

For example, if you want to make a resume template provides us the space in which we can write appropriate data.

> Many times we need table format to represent data. Word processor provides us the facility to insert a table.

> We can insert many types of different shapes into our document with the help of a clip art gallery

> We can insert images in our document.

> we can represent statistical data in many different chart formats like a bar chart, pie chart, circle chart, etc.

> using the page setup option we can set the left margin, right margin, top margin, bottom margin of a document.

> Mail merge is also a very popular feature provided by a word processor.

> spelling and grammar checking is also provided in word processor software. This feature is very useful because of spelling and grammar mistake is very common in writing. Users need not worry about spelling and grammar while typing a document; it automatically corrects it or suggests it

Name of some popular word processor application software

Microsoft Word, word perfect, WordPad, Lotus word Pro, word perfect, Apple works, work pages, open office writer.

Google docs is an online word processor

WPS Office is the most popular Android phone app. This has a word processor, spreadsheet, and PowerPoint presentation features.

(iii) Spreadsheet application

The spreadsheet application is also a very common and important application and it is also a very important application of PC software package.

A spreadsheet is a program that we use to easily perform mathematical calculations on statistical data.

It is also called a formula-based sheet.

There are so many tasks that required formulation. Like calculating percentages, finding the average of a set of numbers, arranging a series of data in acceding or descending order, and many more complex financial and mathematical operations.

In an office, financial institution, bank, railways, school, college, university, and many more areas, formula base documents are required.

For example, in a school, it is used to prepare student mark sheets. Where sum of different subject marks has to be calculated in a particular place of a document, this is done automatically by a spreadsheet application. The user has to be just entering the marks and the sheet will automatically calculate the sum and whatever the user desired. All things are done with the help of formulas.

It is Very common application software in a financial institution. Its biggest advantage is that it helps a lot in data analysis.

Features of spreadsheet application

--- Charts--Like MS Word, it can be used to represent data with the help of various types of charts, but in this, charts are formula-based. Charts get automatically changed according to chart data in a spreadsheet.

---Inserting formulas--

In a spreadsheet application mostly two types of formula can be inserted the first one is template based and the second is user-defined.

[] Template-based-formula

Using the template-based formula we can directly insert the format of the formula. We have to just put the values in an appropriate place and get the result. We need not worry about remembering many many different types of formulas used in banking areas, School areas, financial areas, mathematical areas, and so on.

[] User-defined formulas

It may possible that template-based formulas are not sufficient. In some situations, we need a formula that is not available in the template of the spreadsheet, so the spreadsheet application allows us to set our own formula, with the help of this; we can create any propagation formula. Once the formula is made not only we can use it but also save it into a template for further use.

--- Automatic data generation--

With the help of the spreadsheet application, we do not need to interchange the series of data again and again, as if we are writing the table of 2 we need to write only 2 4, and 6 and then just drag the series till 20. So we can say that table of any number can be written automatically. Such type of many more operations can be done in a spreadsheet application.

(iv) Browser

It is very popular and important software of any modern PC software package. Today we cannot imagine a computer system without the internet. The browser provides us the facility to access many features of the internet.

Browser is special software that is used to access the internet.

It also comes with an operating system. We can also install it separately but most of the operating system provides it free.

Any Browser provides us the following features

---- Net surfing. It is a very very common function provided by a browser. In net surfing, we can just go on a particular website and get the information and switch from one page to another page. This function is known as net surfing

----Email. Email is the second most common feature of the internet. So with the help of a browser, we can access this facility using the email we can send emails to appropriate recipients electronically. And there are so many other features are available in the email. nowadays in mobile phones a separate application is also used for email but using a browser we can definitely access email services .there are also some other messaging software are also used but they cannot be used with the help of browsers like WhatsApp and telegram. These do not email these are just messaging applications. Email is a standard and legal mail service

----Downloading: we can transfer files from one computer to another computer .this is possible due to downloading feature. We can download files or folders from a server to our computer. This is done by internet and browser.

---- Uploading: We can also send our files to the server. Sending the file, data, or folder to the server is called uploading. This is also a very common and useful function of the internet so with the help of Browser we can also do this very easily.

---- E-commerce E-commerce is a modern online method of doing business. It provides a new platform for customers, consumers as well as businessmen. It changed the retail sector.

With the help of Browser, we can also access the facilities of e-commerce.

----Online multimedia platform: Many websites like YouTube provides us the facility of watching online videos and listing to music. And these multimedia platforms can be accessed from any web browser.

-----> Google chrome, internet explorer, Mozilla Firefox, opera mini is the name of some popular browsers.

3.2 DISK OPERATING SYSTEM (DOS)

DOS is a personal computer operating system designed and developed by Microsoft Corporation.

It is very one of the oldest operating system used in personal computers. It provides a character based interface. It means whatever we want to do we have to enter appropriate commands. It provides a character user interface (CUI).

It is also called CUI based operating system.

It is a command based operating system. Command is a set of characters. The meanings of these commands are stored in already loaded dos files. Everything is done by these commands in DOS.

Because of its interface (CUI), it is not very popular. Working on DOS is comparatively harder than windows which are based on GUI (graphical user interface). But still, it has some powerful features. Many sophisticated users (not ordinary computer users) like it more.

It is a single-user operating system. This means at a particular time of movement only one user can access a computer.

DOS command

DOS provides a variety of commands to perform various tasks related to computers.

With the help of the DOS command, we can display a list of all files and directories on a particular part of a disk, create new files and remove directories, unwanted files and directories, and more.

DOS command can be entered either in uppercase or lowercase letters. The format of the DOS command is called syntax. DOS command is like a math formula where we have to put the appropriate values at an appropriate place to get the results.

To use DOS, first of all, we have to know all the commands of DOS. Let us discuss some DOS commands.

Directory commands

A directory is a place where we can store our files. Basically, a directory is like a folder but in the DOS folder term is not used. Here the task of the folder is to be done by directory. In this section, we are going to see different directory related commands

- i DIR command

This command is used to show list of files or directories stored in current drive.

Syntax

C\> DIR <Enter>

To do use this command you have to just type DIR and press enter key from the keyboard. It will show all files and directories of the C drive. C drive is a portion of the hard disk.

- - ii MD command

This command is used to make a new directory.

Syntax

C:\>MD <directory name> <Enter>

Example\

C:\>MD varanasi <Enter>

With this command, a new directory named Varanasi will be created.

--- iii RD command

This command is used to remove a directory.

Syntax

C:\>RD <directory name> <Enter>

Example\

C:\>RD varanasi <Enter>

With this command, a directory named Varanasi will be removed.

--- iv CD command

This command is used to change a directory.

Syntax

C:\>CD <directory name> <Enter>

Example\

C:\> CD Varanasi <Enter>

With this command, the current directory will change from c: to C:\varansai. After this, we will in the Varanasi directory.

File command

i. Copy con

This command is used to make a new file

Syntax

C:\>copy con <file name>

Example:

C:\>copy con file1

Here file1 is a new file name that we want to make. After this write the content of the file and after that press, ctrl+z to save the file.

i. Copy

This command is used to Copies and appends files.

Syntax

COPY <Source drive>: (File spec 1) <Target drive>: (File spec 2)

Where Source drive refers to the drive from where the file has to be copied.
Example:
Copy c:\file1 d:\file2
After this file1 is to be copied into drive d with name file2

iii. type

This command is used to display the content of a file.
Syntax
C:> type<filename> <enter>
Example
C:> type file1 <enter>
It will show the content of file1.

iv. REN

This command is used rename the filename
Syntax
C:> ren <oldfilename><newfilename> <enter>
Example
C:> ren <file1><file2> <enter>
This command will change the file name of file1 with file2.
Some More DOS Commands

i. Date command it is used to show or change the current date of system

Syntax
C:> date<enter >

ii. time command it is used to show or change the current time of system

Syntax
C:> time <enter >

iii. cls command it is used to clear the screen

Syntax
C :> cls <enter >

iv. The ECHO Command it is used to print a message on the screen

Syntax
C:> echo " hello welcome in the world of computer " <enter >

v. Prompt it is used to Change the DOS command prompt.

Syntax
C:\> PROMPT pg <Enter>

Example

C:\>PROMPT hello pg <Enter>

The above command will display the following prompt:

hello C: \>_

Internal and External Commands

All DOS commands can be classified into two main categories: Internal Commands and External Commands.

Internal Commands

Commands that are part of the core files of DOS (COMMAND.COM) are known as internal commands. They are loaded in the computer main memory as soon as the computer is on running mode. The important internal commands are DIR, COPY, DEL, REN, MD, CD, RD, TYPE,

COPY CON, DATE, TIME, CLS, ECHO, PROMPT, and PATH. These commands are very commonly and frequently used.

External Commands

External commands are those commands which are not stored in the computer's main memory. It is stored in disks as separate program files. The extension of these files is either COM or EXE. These commands are not frequently used commands. These commands are not very common and it is used for some specific purpose.

The commonly used external commands are FORMAT, DISKCOPY, CHKDSK, XCOPY, and LABEL.

Various DOS versions

The latest version of DOS is MS-DOS6. 22 released in 1994. , MS-DOS (Microsoft), Apple DOS, Dr-DOS, PC-DOS (IBM).

Note: DOS commands are not case sensitive. Means there is no difference between capital letter and small letters.

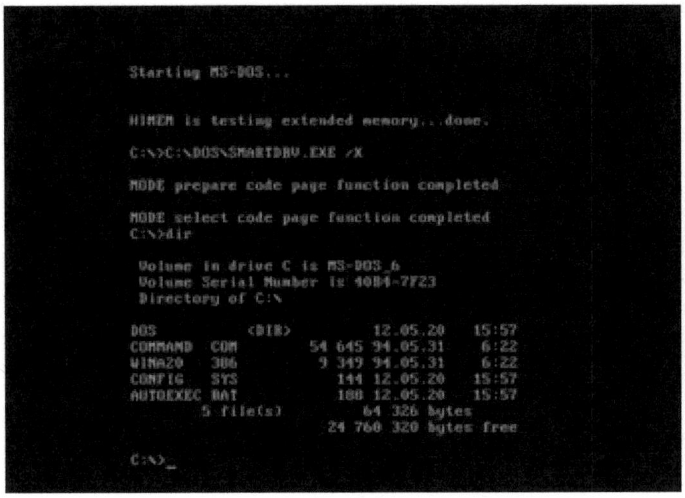

Fig: A sample DOS screen

3.3 WINDOWS

Windows is an operating system developed by Microsoft Corporation.

It is a very popular operating system for a desktop computer or personal computer.

It is a very user-friendly operating system. It means that working on Windows provides a very easy environment for the user.

As we know that providing an interface is an important function of an operating system so Windows is also an Operating System and it provides a very e easy interface for its uses.

Interference of Windows operating system is so convenient that even a 10-year-old child can easily use a complex system such as a computer. This is the biggest feature of the operating system of Windows operating system. It would not be wrong to say here that the Windows operating system has so much popularity because of the interface. And at the same time, we can also say that the secret of the success of the Windows operating system is its interface design.

Windows is a GUI (graphical user interface) based operating system. it has been designed how to make our work more convenient and easy. In a DOS-based operating system, we have to remember a lot of commands to perform any task but Windows operating system provides us a graphical based interface in which we do not need to remember all these commands. In Windows, everything is provided in the form of pictures and graphics.

Basically, Windows operating system comes with a special device, called Mouse. Using Mouse a user can navigate throughout the screen select and execute the appropriate program, folder and perform many many desirable tasks.

Selecting folder selecting text drag and drop right-clicking double-clicking are some common functions of mouse coma these are some common functions of the mouse. With the help of mouse functions, working in the Windows operating system has become very easy and convenient. The user who once works in Windows operating system uses FIR DOS operating system; I find it very hard to work.

Windows versions

Windows98, Windows2000, Windows XP, windows7, and windows8 are some most popular operating systems.

Windows 10 is the latest operating system.

Windows has many versions, all have different features, but when we talk about Windows here; we talk about a common Windows operating system. Let's talk about such features which are found in almost all versions.

Hardware Requirements

The minimum hardware configuration required to run Windows 98 is given below:

-1 GHz- 2.6 GHz processor based CPU

-125 MB - 1 GB of RAM

-40 GB to 1 TB free disk space

-LCD/LED monitor-

-Mouse

-Keyboard

Benefits and features of Windows

-- Windows provide a graphical interface.

-- All the programs are shown in the form of icons. So it is very easy to access any program. To access a program you have to just double click on the appropriate program.

-- it has an inbuilt copy of MS-Dos. So if any user is familiar with DOS he can easily use dos with windows.

-- It is a multitasking Operating System. It means that in Windows users can perform multiple tasks simultaneously. For example, you can write on MS Word in the meanwhile you can also listen to music using media player and also give a print command to print a document and also can download a file from the internet.

-- It has plug-and-play features. Using plug and play feature Windows automatically detects some additional peripheral devices. It can detect any additional hardware automatically and then install the proper drivers for a particular device. For example, I want to use a new Mouse so we don't need to worry about the driver software. I just plug the wire of the mouse into the USB port and Windows automatically detect the driver and we can start the use of the device.

-- It provides us desktop. A desktop is a place where we can put our frequently used programs, files, or folders. Basically desktop is the name of the first appearing screen that is present when a computer is starting.

-- In Windows operating system we can also connect some other computers to it using the network neighborhood option.

-- Windows also supports all the latest versions of Browser using that we can access the internet facility.

-- Windows provide system tools. Using this function Windows users can maintain their system themselves.

-- Windows has a lot of security features. It provides authenticity. This means that only authentic users can access the system. Authenticity is done by a password. Without a password, no one can access the system.

-- Windows provide a searching facility. This is a very common task a user required. We can find an appropriate file, folder or program if forget the location and even the full name.

Desktop

A desktop is an integrated place of Windows. It is a space where we can organize programs, folders, and documents, which appear as icons. Our desktop is always in the background, behind any other applications you're running.

It is the first screen that appears when we start the windows. Background icons and the taskbar appears on the desktop. From this place, we can access the installed program from the start menu, or by double-clicking any application shortcut.

Fig: windows7 Desktop

Note: You can access your desktop at any time by pressing windowkey+d

Device Manager

Device Manager shows all hardware devices attached to the computer. With this help, we can know which hardware is installed on our computer. With the help of the Device Manager option, we can view, update and uninstall hardware drivers.

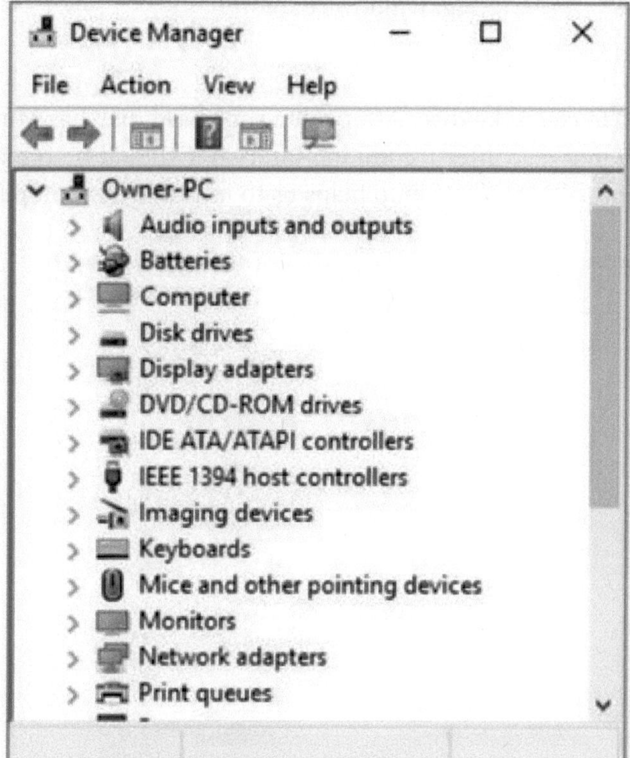

Fig: device manager option

Windows Explorer

Window Explorer is also called File Explorer.

It provides us the facility of viewing files and folders on the computer. Basically, Windows Explorer provides us an integrated place from where we can access our different storage devices. Generally, our files or folders are stored in a particular area of the disc. It may be a hard disk, pen drive, CD /DVD drive, or any other removable disk. Therefore all types of storage areas can be accessed through File Explorer.

The shortcut key of Window Explorer is Window + E.

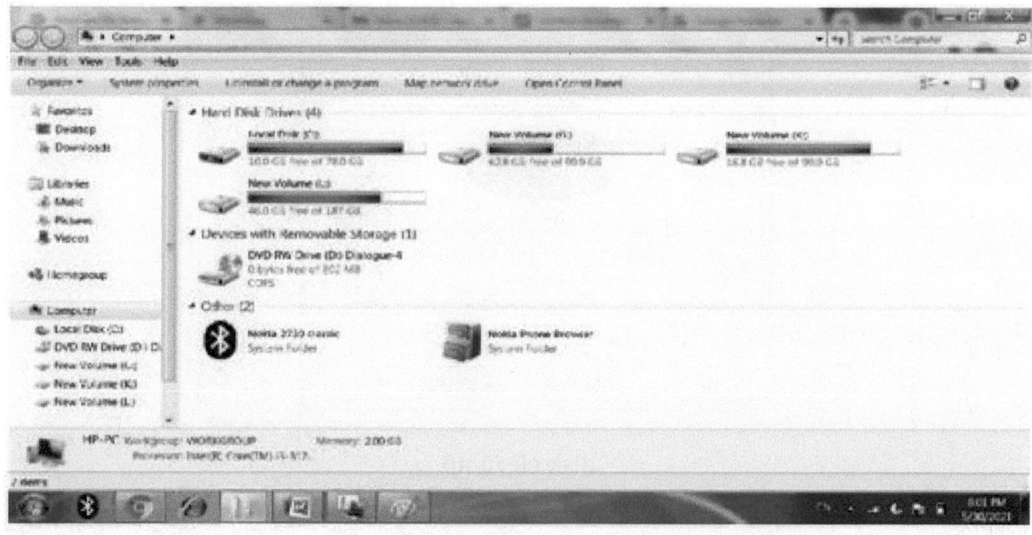

Fig: windows explorer

Disk cleanup

The disk cleanup program is used to clean the disc. After some time hard disk has Mini temporary files and these files occupying a large amount of memory .so after a common interval it should be removed. So Windows provides us the facility to clean up the disk manually. Disk cleanup helps us to improve our computer's performance.

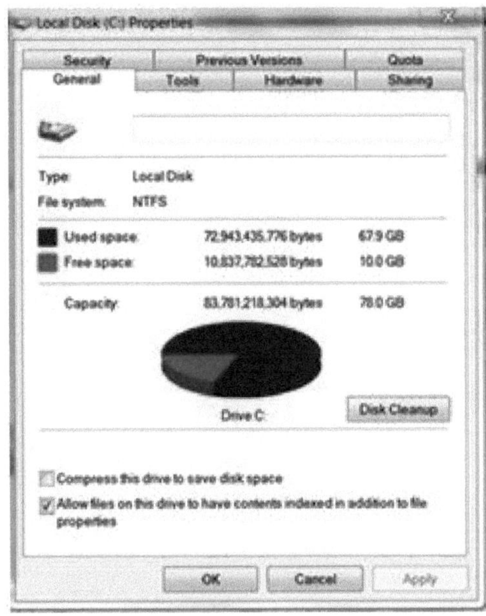

disk clean up

To access disk clean up option

1. select desired drive for example c:
2. right click and select properties option
3. On the general tab select Disk Cleanup option.

Internet Explorer

Enter Caption

Internet Explorer is a browser and as we know a browser is software that is used to access the internet facility. Many internet-related tasks like net surfing, emailing, downloading, watching movies, game playing and many more things can be accessed through internet explorer. We can also install other browsers but Internet Explorer is a default browser of the Windows operating system.

To access internet explorer just click on internet explorer icon appear on desktop.

Microsoft paint

Microsoft paint is also called MS Paint. It is a very popular application program for drawing coloring and painting. Using MS Paint we can also edit images. Freehand drawing is a unique feature of MS Paint. In MS Paint, we can do drawing and painting exactly as we do with copy and pen in real life, the pen work is done by the mouse and the copy work is done by the screen. The default extension of paint file is .bmp but it also supports many other image formats like .jpeg, jpg, .gif, .png, .tiff.

To access MS-Paint, double-click the Paint option on the desktop or from the Start menu.

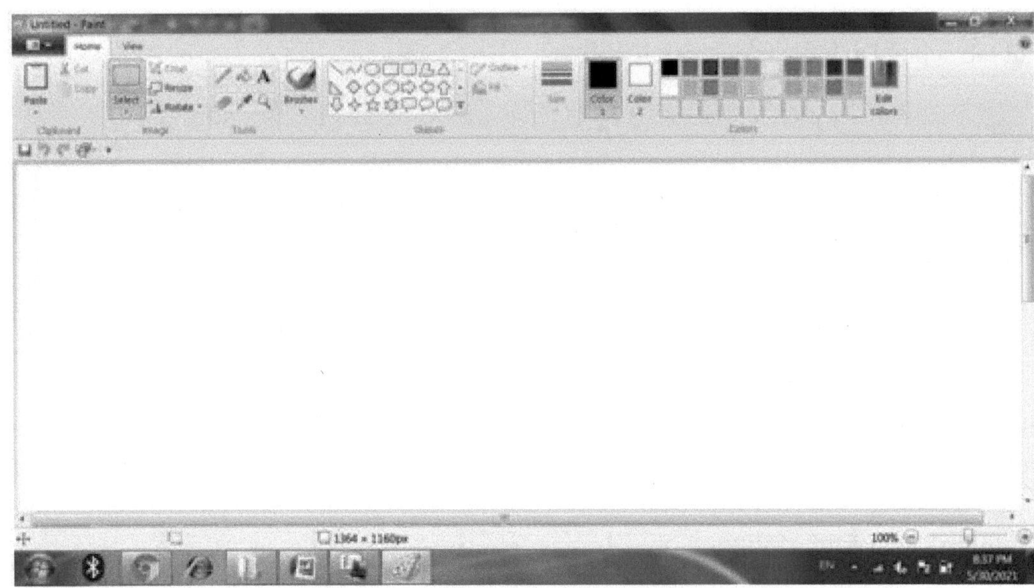

Fig: MS-paint window

Notepad

Notepad is a text editor. It is a default text editor comes with any windows operating system. Using Text Editor we can create, edit or remove any text files. Extension of notepad file is .txt.

To open Notepad, click on the Notepad option from Start Menu > Programs > Notepad.

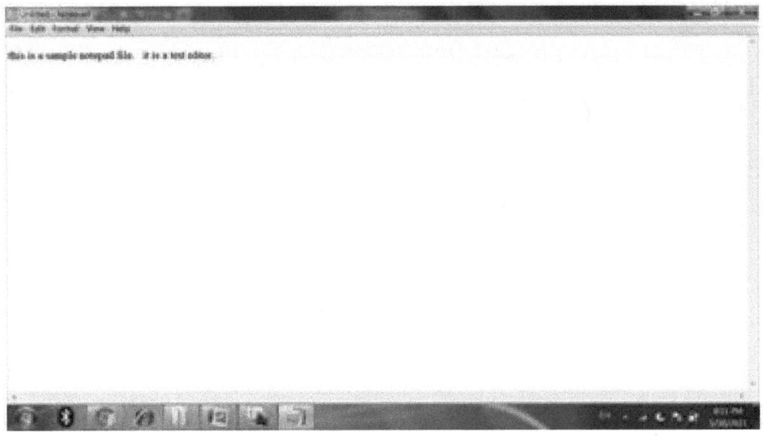

Fig: notepad file.

Control panel

The Control panel is a very important option for the Windows operating system.

With the help of the control panel, we can adjust the settings of different computer components. for example display setting, folder options, screen color management, audio setting, user account setting, credential manager, device manager, internet setting, mouse setting, keyboard setting, date and time setting, network setting, backup and restore, etc.

To access goto start > control panel

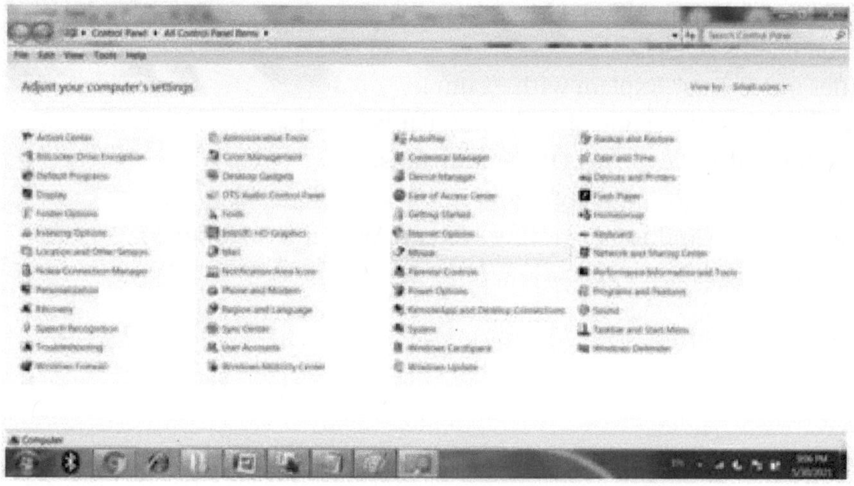

Fig: control panel of windows

Network

Like many other task computers, can also communicate with other computers. To provide this facility network option is available in Windows. Using this option we can send a file folder to another computer without using the internet. It is a very useful option for file sharing.

To access this just click on the network option that appears on the network icon.

Exercises

Objective type question

Choose the correct answer for the followings

1. Which of the following software can't be categorized as application software?
(a) Driver software (b) MS-DOS (c) Spreadsheet (c) Word processing
2. Which of the following software is not an important part of any pc software package?
(a) Operating system (b) DBMS (c) Spreadsheet (d) Word processing
3. ___________ enables users to perform different types of activities and work that computers were designed for.
(a) System Software (b) Application Software (c) Device Software (e) None of these
4. A group of software programs bundled into a single package is called
(a) Combination Software (b) A Software Suite (c) A software Package (d) A software Collection
5. Browser is an example of
(a) Input device (b) driver software (c) internet access software (d) output device
6. DOS is ------------- based operating system
(a) GUI (b) CUI (c) touch screen (d) voice-based
7. CLS command in DOS is used for
(a) Shut down (b) booting (c) make a file (d) clear the screen
8. to open windows explorer which of the following shortcut key combination is used?
(a) window+E (b) ctrl+H (c) ctrl+G (d) ctrl+E
9. The extension of paintbrush application is
(a) .txt (b) .mp4 (c) .mp3 (d) .bmp
10. Spreadsheet application is mainly used for
(a) Sound editing (b) photo editing (c) formula based sheet (d) design sheet

Theoretical questions

1. Describe the term PC Software Package in detail.
2. What is an operating system? Define MS-DOS.
3. List some directory commands of DOS.
4. How will you copy files in Ms-Dos? Explain with example.
5. What do mean by browser? List the name of some popular browsers.
6. Differentiate between internal and external DOS commands.
7. What are the functions of word processor software?
8. List the striking features of the windows operating system? Why it is so famous?
9. Write a short note on the spreadsheet application.

CHAPTER FOUR

Database Concept

in this chapter, we are going to focus on computer data in reference to business. But before it first let us know some basic terms related to database and business data processing.

4.1 Data and information:

A computer is a data processor. The basic function of the Computer is to Store data that comes after processing. As we know the computer is an electronic device. It takes the data process is under the program and generates information. So, first of all, you have to know what is data and information.

Data: any raw fact is called data. In other words, we can say unprocessed fact is called data.

Data may be in the form of character, letter, word, audio, images and even in video format. Data is of no use to us unless it is useful to us.

Information: processed data is called information. In other words, we can say that processed fact is called information. Information is meaningful for us.

If seen, the main function of a computer is to convert data into information. For this reason, it is called a data processor, it converts data into information. Because data is of no use to us and information is very important to us, that's why the computer was invented. Computers can process thousands of times more data than humans, that too in thousands of times less time. Computer processing tasks can be divided into three-part first take input data second perform processing and third produce output.

INPUT ------------------------> PROCESS -----------------------------------> OUTPUT

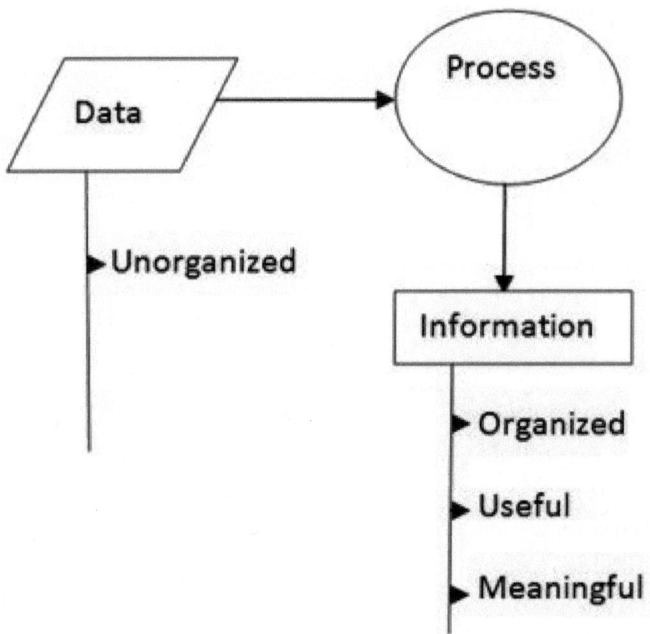

Fig: data and information

Processing is the job of a computer. But it depends on input data and output data. Data must be either display or to be stored for further use. So ultimately everything is dependent on data, whether it is input or output.

So data storage becomes a highly important issue because if we kept it in a good manner we can save a much processing time for computers as well users (human beings).to do this we need some special program which can take care of data before and after processing. Or we can say that we need a program that is completely dedicated to data and only data.

4.2 Business Data Processing

In computer terminology data means an electric signal, bits and bytes, and so on. But if this computer data belongs to any business operation it becomes money. For example, binary data that just belong to an operating system command, and if it is lost or not executed within time; need not worry, just reenter the command. But what happens if the data belongs to any financial operation; and if it is lost, here we cannot say that data is lost. There is a loss of money.

So it is very important to know one thing that there is a difference between normal computer data and business data in a computer. Therefore this process involving business data processing such as storing, sorting, searching, selecting, updating, etc. should be changed. It requires a special method to perform all the related tasks in an optimized manner. Database is one of them.

Business data processing involves a series of operations that converts all unorganized business data into meaningful information that can help to take appropriate decisions. Basically, it is an analysis process of finding some useful information on the basis of limited available raw data. It is a power of data processing system that how to find this valuable information using less time and high accuracy. We can say that the success of any business organization is depending on effective uses of business data processing.

Today generally all business organization uses a database system to manage business data. So let's know about the database.

4.3 Database:

A database is an organized collection of related information.

A database is a set of interdependent data of a particular entity.

A database is not just a collection of records but an arrangement of records in such a way that it can be easily managed. For example, records of students in a school, records of employees in an office, details of account holders in a bank, telephone directory, etc.

Database structure:

character character character character

Field

Field Field Field Field

Record

Record Record Record Record

File

File File File File

Databse

Character: This is the basic building block of data. It includes alphabets (a,b,c.........A,B,C.....),numbers(0,1,2,....),special symbols (@, #,$,%,......). We can say that it is a smallest unit of any data.

Field: a meaningful group of related characters.

Record: a meaningful group of related Fields.

File: a meaningful group of related records.

Database: a set of integrated and related files.

Here a sample student database is given to better understand the term.

FILE 1 :STUDENT BASIC RECORDS

SR. NO. ROLL NUMBER NAME FATHER'S NAME DATE OF BIRTH CITY MOB.
1 21108001 AJAY KUMARNEELKANTH KUMAR 12/5/2001 VARANASI -
2 21108002 VIKAS YADAV RAMASHISH YADAV 27/12/2000 PRAYAGRAJ-
3 21108003 SUNEL SINGH DEV NARAYAN SINGH 1/5/1999 VARANASI-
4 21108004 MOH. ABDUL KHAN NUR ABDUL 8/8/2002 BALLIA-
5 2110800 KISHORAWASHTIRAJSHEKHARAWASTHI12/1/2001AZAMGARH
6 21108006 ACHINTYASINGHALBRIJMOHAN SINGHAL29/09/2000KANPUR
7 21108007 SHREYA GUPTA KRISHNA GUPTA 28/05/2002 JAUNPUR -
8 21108008 KESHAW PANDEY DEEPAK PANDEY 3/6/2000 GAZIABAD -
9 21108009 ROHAN VERMA KAILASH VERMA 31/12/2002 VARANASI -

FILE 2:STUDENT CURRENT RECORD

SR. NO. ROLL NUMBER CURRENT YEAR SUBJECT STREAM PREVIOUSRESULT
1 21108001 FIRST YEAR COMMERCE PASSED
2 21108002 FIRST YEAR COMMERCE PASSED
3 21108003 FIRST YEAR COMMERCE PASSED
4 21108004 FIRST YEAR COMMERCE PASSED
5 21108005 FIRST YEAR COMMERCE PASSED
6 21108006 FIRST YEAR COMMERCE PASSED
7 21108007 FIRST YEAR COMMERCE PASSED
8 21108008 FIRST YEAR COMMERCE PASSED
9 21108009 FIRST YEAR COMMERCE PASSED

FILE 3:STUDENT QUALIFYING EXAM RECORD

SR. NO. ROLL NUMBER QUALIFYING EXAM SUBJECT STREAM MARKS OBTAINED TOTAL MARKS
1 21108001 10+2 COMMERCE 410 500
2 21108002 10+2 COMMERCE 425 500
3 21108003 10+2 COMMERCE 450 500
4 21108004 10+2 SCIENCE 880 1000
5 21108005 10+2 COMMERCE 390 500
6 21108006 10+2 COMMERCE 389 500
7 21108007 10+2 SCIENCE 890 1000
8 21108008 10+2 COMMERCE 405 500
9 21108009 10+2 COMMERCE 419 500

> Database name: student
> Student database consist three files
> File1: Student Basic Records.

Fields (7): Sr. no., Roll number, Name, Father's_name,Date_of_Birth, City and mob.
Record (1): 1 21108001 ajay kumar neelkanth kumar 12/5/2001 varanasi -
Record (2): 2 21108002 vikas yadav ramashish yadav 27/12/2000 prayagraj -
......
......
......
Record (9): 9 21108009 rohan verma kailash verma 31/12/2002 varanasi -

> File 2: Student Current Record
> File 3: Student Qualifying Exam Record

As we can see file 1 has 7 fields (number, roll number, name, father's name, date of birth, city, crowd). Each field has 9 records. All the fields are related to each other and all the records belong to the same entity i.e. student parent record. For example, roll number 21108001 belongs to "Ajay Kumar" who belongs to Varanasi city.

In File2: Student Current Record there are 5 fields i.e. serial number, roll number, current year, subject stream, and previous results, and a total of 9 records. In this file, other information about students is stored. Through this file, we can get information about student's current records. If you want to know what is the subject stream of a particular student? On the basis of roll number, we can get this record from this file.

File3: Student Qualifying Exam, the record has 6 fields i.e. serial number, roll number, qualifying exam subject stream, marks obtained, total marks, and 9 records. This file gives the qualifying exam record of a particular student. If you want to know what were the student marks obtained in his qualifying exam? Then we can get this information from this record.

Finally, the student database consists of these three files. These three files are combinedly known as databases. we can get any kind of record whether it belongs to student basic record or student current record or student qualify exam record .whenever we want to combine all this information into a single place we can get them from these three files using the database. That is the advantage of a database that there is a separate existence of each file but combinedly we can get the information. For example, if we want to know Ajay Kumar is pass or not? We can get the roll number from file 1 that is 211082001 and then search this roll number into file 2 and get that he is pass or fail. So the database provides us information about Ajay Kumar that he is pass or not. in the same way, if you want to know that what was the marks obtained of Ajay Kumar in the 10+2 qualifying exam so in the same way we can get the roll number of Ajay Kumar from file 1 and from file 3 research the selected roll number and get the marks that are 410.

All data are stored in a very organized way. Because whenever we want to search a record for a particular student we can easily find them. And even all related data can also be found because they are all arranged in a proper way.

Note: in general writing practice only the 'DATA' term has been used, rather than information.

Properties of a database:

--- A database is a logical collection of data with some meaning.

--- Individual data in a database has no meaning. Every set of data of a database is related to another set of databases. Random Collection of data cannot be said to be a database.

--- Designing a database has a specific purpose.

--- Databases are generally related to the real world.

--- Databases are commonly used in business applications.

--- The database is generally represented in the form of tables. The table contains rows and columns.

Column referred as a field, row as a record and table is called an entity in the database.

--- Every record must belong to the table. And all fields must be interrelated.

The basic problem of the file system is a dependency on the application program. So first of all data must be separated from an application program. We can say that application programs play the role of interface between user and data. Basically, without an application program, we cannot access data. This is known as data dependency on the application program. For example, if we work on ms-excel and save the file for future access. Suppose we want to use this file elsewhere. To access the file in some other place (on another computer), ms –excel must be installed on that place (computer). This means without ms-excel we cannot access that file. Whenever we want to access that file we need ms-excel.

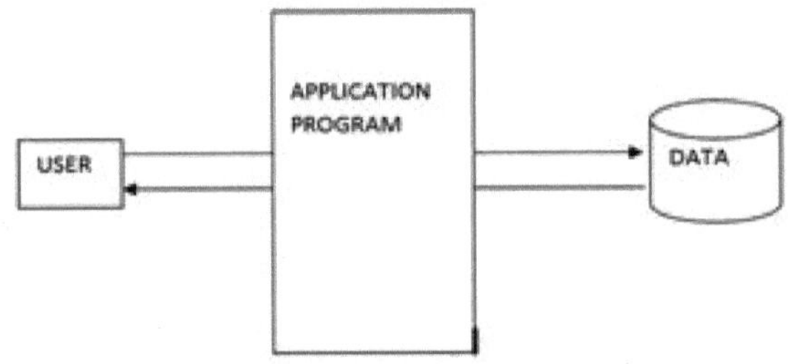

Fig: data access in file system

In a database, data is separate from the application programs. Data is not dependant on any particular application pregame. Data can be accessed from many programs.

Data is a separate entity in the database. In terms of database, this separate and consolidated entity of data is called schema. The database has not only data but it is a collection of many elements.

Schema is a logical relationship between these various elements of the database. Basically, the schema itself is an important component of the overall database. With the help of schema, any program that wants to access the data can generate dictionaries that contain a complete description of the database.

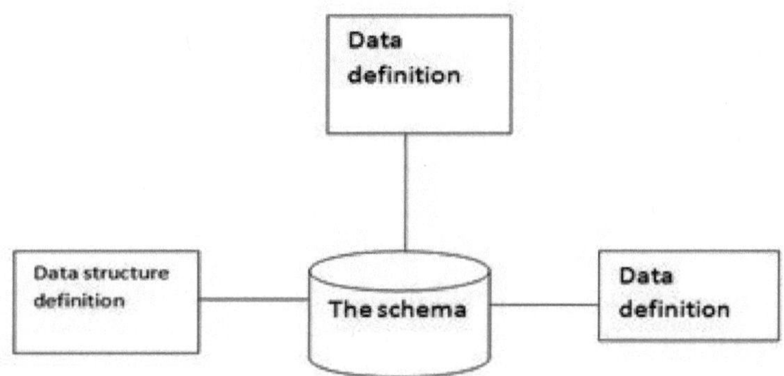

Fig: Database concept

Database administrator

Database systems are typically managed, installed, and controlled by the database administrator. He is responsible for data definitions and standards. He is the main authority to define any technical term that is needed for the overall functionality of a database. The fundamental duties of a database administrator are as follows.

-- Establish and control data definitions and standards.
-- Determining the relationship among data elements.
-- Designing the data-based security system.
-- Documentation of data dictionary.
-- Maintenance of database.
-- Review of schema.

After discussing all things we must have to know the advantages of using a database. Here it is given in a summarized way.

Advantage of database
-- Lack of data redundancy
-- High data security
-- Data independence
-- Data consistency
-- Reduce data storage
-- Easy data sharing.

4.4 Database vs. File system

File system

A file system is a system of storing the data in an organized way by the operating system of a computer.

In other words, a "file system is a system that is used to manage the files of the system."

File (file):-

A file is a group of related information that is stored in secondary storage such as - Magnetic disc, optical disc, etc. Any kind of data can be stored in the file like- text, image, audio or video, etc.

File access methods

The method by which the information stored in the files is accessed.

Following are the file access methods:-

i:- sequential access

ii:- direct access

iii:- indexed sequential access

i:- Sequential Access:- In sequential access, the information present in the file is accessed in a sequence. That is, the information is accessed one after the other in sequence.

Like: - We have a file which has 3 records- a b c

So we will access a first, then b then c. In this method, we cannot access b first or c first. For example, if the plates are placed one above the other on the dining table, then to take the last plate, you can take a plate from top to bottom in order. No plate can pass through the middle.

ii:- Direct access:- Direct access is also called random access.

Through direct access, we can directly access any information present in the file. Through this, we can access the file very fast. Each information in the file has its own address, so with the help of that address, it is directly accessed for reading and writes.

For example, if we want to take one of the glasses filled with water on the dining table, then we can take any glass directly. We are not required to follow the sequence.

This method is commonly used in databases.

iii:- Indexed sequential access:- This method has been made on the basis of sequential access. In this, an index is created for each file which keeps pointers for different blocks. In this, the index is used to control the pointer while accessing the file.

A database is a modern approach but a Traditional file system is still commonly used today. But there are so many drawbacks to this system.

Limitations of traditional file system approach

Data redundancy: data redundancy means duplicate data present in multiple files. The basic data fields are used in many different files. For example, suppose file1 containing student detail and if all or two or more data fields are used in file 2 i.e. name along with roll number. Roll number is necessary for file 2 for relation establishment to file 1. But what is the need for a name again in file 2? In a file system, two files cannot be interconnected so the problem of data redundancy occurs. In short, we can say that in file systems data can be repeated again and again in many files and there is no provision to check it. Due to which the memory is wasted

Data inconsistency: data inconsistency means field values must be the same if they belong to the same field no matter they are situated in a single file or multiple. When changes are made in a data item every file which contains that field must be changed. Confusion can result when one file has newly updated data with another file containing the same field that has old not updated data .this is a very general situation and lead to the problem of inconsistency.

Data independence: in a file system, a program that is used to maintain files has some specifications. The file format in which we store the data, we also need the same file format to access the data, this is called data dependency. For example, we will always need MS Excel to open the .xls file of EXCEL format, in this way our Excel data is always needed for the application program. So in order to access the data, we have to install that application program in the system, so that the application program whose data is there in the file system, there is an additional problem of the installation of the application program in a file system.

Difference between the file system and the database

DATABASE is a collection of data. In this, users do not need to write procedures. A file system is also a collection of data but users need to write procedures in it.

-- Database is system software that manages data.

The file system is also software, but it manages the data files together with the operating system in the computer system.

-- DATABASE provides an abstract view of the data. Due to which the details remain hidden.

The file system provides the details of the representation of the data and the storage of the data.

-- DATABASE has more security features than a file system.

-- DATABASE is very easy to update, select and search the data because SQL query is used in it. The functions of store, search, retrieve, etc. are done manually in the file system, so it is difficult to manage the data in it.

-- The repetition of data is prevented in a database, but it is not so in the file system, the same data is used again and again, due to which the memory is wasted.

-- The process of backup and recovery in a database is very difficult. The process of backup and recovery is easy in the file system.

-- Database is suitable for multiple users. A file system is suitable for a single user.

DATABASE example: MS-Access, MySQL, MSSQL, Oracle, DB2, etc.

File system Example: - NTFS, FAT, Ext, etc.

Exercises

Objective type question

Choose the correct answer for the followings.

1. Which of the following is best suitable term to define 'data'?
(a) Processed fact (b) any meaningful fact (c) useful fact (d) raw fact
2. Which of the following is best suitable term to define 'information'?
(a) Processed fact (b) unprocessed fact (c) meaningless data (d) raw fact
3. Database is a collection of -------------------- information
(a) Useless (b) related (c) many (d) collected
4. Database is a
(a) Collection of related files (b) a device to store data (c) text editor (d) word processor
5. In term of database record is a collection of
(a) Field (b) character (c) data (d) fact
6. In term of database field is a collection of
(a) Data (b) character (c) record (d) fact
7. File data is based on
(a) Application program (b) system call (c) driver software (d) none of these
8. Schema is a
(a) Fact
(b) Physical component of database
(c) Record in a file
(d) Logical relationship between various components of database
9. An example of a database is
(a) MS-Excel (b) notepad (c) MS-Access (d) .mp4
10. Which of the following is an important advantage of database?
(a) Storage technique (b) lack of data redundancy (c) data dependency (d) schema

Theoretical questions

1. What do you mean by Business Data Processing? Explain in detail.
2. Differentiate between data and information.
3. Describe the term database. List some properties of the database.
4. What are the functions of a database administrator?
5. Compare database system with a traditional file system.
6. With the help of an example explain a database term 'schema'.
7. Design a database for a banking organization with appropriate fields and records.

8. Explain different types of file access methods.
9. What do you understand by the database administrator? List their responsibilities.

CHAPTER FIVE

DBMS (DATABASE MANAGEMENT SYSTEM)

In the previous chapter, we have discussed the concept of only a database. Now next we will talk about some of the programs used to access the database.

In this chapter, we are going to discuss the database management system and its type.

5.1 Overview of DBMS

When we talk about databases, our main focus is to store the data. But only storage of data is not sufficient. We have to use some special type of mechanism through which we can access that particular data in an efficient way.

We can understand Database Management System by dividing it into two main parts. The first part is to store the data and the second part is to access the data. There is some mechanism in storing and some different mechanism is used in accessing. The system used to store the data can be included in the database. Whereas the system used to access the data is called DBMS. We can understand this better with the help of an example.

We can use the library of a university to understand the database management system. If seen, the database management system i.e. DBMS is similar to the library of a very big university, the books of that library work in the manner of a database.

Library books are in the way of data in DBMS. The description of those books, such as the title of the book, the name of its author, the name of the publication, its price, etc. is called a database. Library examples are very effective for understanding DBMS because if we do not maintain this entire library system properly then it becomes very difficult to manage them. Books are the same but when we do not keep them in a systematic way then it becomes very difficult to access, manage them and if we keep them systematically in a particular standard way then we can manage them easily. Library books are kept in a special way. Normally we do not understand it, but the person who knows that particular method can easily access those books. If we do not keep the library books in a systematic order then accessing those books will become a very complicated process. To ease this complex process, libraries around the world have a standard system (this is what library science teaches) on how to store books. It sounds very easy to hear or read, but when we imagine a very big library, then it becomes necessary for us to be aware of that arrangement here. It is not a matter of an ordinary person to find a book from the library or to keep the books there in a systematic order. It is very clear to say that we need some specialized standard system to keep and find books in the library. This saves a lot of money, time, and labor. Database Management System is also the name of this systematic sequence which we do to store and access data on a computer.

We can also divide the database management system into two parts such as the library system. Just like the first books come in the library and they have to be kept in a particular order, similarly in the DBMS also, first of all, the data has to be stored in a particular arrangement. When the books come to the library, the main task of the librarian and its main purpose is to keep the books at a particular place under the pre-determined arrangement, to attach some additional information on those books, which is called accession number, in the same way in DBMS also, when new data is inserted, it uses some additional information attached with the data, which is called data description. The task becomes much easier once the books are put in a systematic order. In the future, if a student demands a book, the librarian searches it easily because he knows under which arrangement we have kept it. In the same way, DBMS can easily access the data from the database which is stored on a computer hard disk. It is very clear and simple to say that the work that is in the library of the librarian is in the database of the DBMS.

The way many books are managed in a particular way in the library, in the same way, the data in the computer is also managed through DBMS. Just as there is benefit in keeping the books in a systematic order in the library, in the same way, managing the data in the computer through DBMS also benefits a lot if the books are kept in a very systematic way in the library if they are managed in a particular way. If done in this way, it saves a lot of money, time, and labor, in the same way, if the data is stored and acted on the computer with the help of DBMS, then we save a lot of time. So the summary is that Database Management System is a system that helps us to access the stored data.

5.2 Understanding DBMS:

DBMS is an advanced technique for storing information. It is an advancement of the traditional file system. Basically, DBMS is a special program that is dedicated only and only for data. Each and every function of this program is related to data. Whether to enter new data or to modify it or to add something new or to search for any data or delete data, all these functions come under DBMS.

DBMS = DATABASE MANAGEMENT SYSTEM

DBMS = DATABASE + MANAGEMENT SYSTEM

DBMS = DB + MS

DB = organized collection of related information.

MS= a program to manage DB.

MANAGEMENT SYSTEM: software that is used to manage the database.

So DBMS is a database management system made with two terms DB and Ms. DB means an organized collection of related information and Ms. Means a program to manage that database. So we can say that

DBMS is software used to manage databases.

In computer science, two kinds of operation must be performed to manage data: first store data and second access the data. So first of all at the time of storing the data, we have to follow some mechanism in such a way that it can be accessed in the future easily.

Keeping the data in such a way that it can be easily accessed in future, this technology is called DBMS, while storing the data, we need some special program which helps us to keep the data in such a way that that it can be easily accessed in future. In our given example of the library, there are many thousands of millions of books. When it comes to the library if we don't keep them in an organized way then it will be very difficult to find a particular book in the future. Similarly, the program helps us while storing the data so that any particular data can be done easily in the future.

dBase, My Sql,Ms-Access and oracle are some popular dbms program.

5.3 DBMS: a standard definition

DBMS is a collection of programs to store and retrieve data from a database.

DBMS is a software package that is used to manage databases.

DBMS is an interface between user and database. With the help of DBMS, a user can perform various database operations such as storage, creation, updating, retrieval, deletion, or protection of the database.

In other words, "DBMS is a software application that is used to create, access, and manage databases."

It acts as an interface between the user and the database. There are many commands in this, through which the user can easily do all the operations related to the database. In other words, we can say that "DBMS is what acts as an interface between end-users and database. So that the data is organized in an orderly manner and can be accessed easily."

After discussing all things, finally, we can say that it is a general-purpose software system that provides us with the following features:-

i. Data Definition – It is used to create, delete and modify the definition defining the organization of the database. It contains detailed descriptions of data. It is used before data insertion in the database.

What type of data will be what will be its length and any special rules related to data, should be decided in advance before inserting the data? Because later it is not possible after there is a record difference. This eliminates the possibility of data-related mistakes in the future. For example, suppose the roll number of a student is to be entered and the roll number of the student concerned contains only numeric values, then in the definition of the data or already fixed that there in the field of roll number only the number Can only insert If a user enters the alphabet in the column of roll number, then the database management system will refuse it.

ii. Data Updating – It is used to insert, delete, and modify the actual data in the database. After the data is inserted, there is a possibility of mistakes in it or after some time the record which was entered becomes outdated, so there should also be a facility to change the inserted record, so this facility is provided in the database management system. Once a record is entered, later we can change, edit, update or delete it.

iii. Data Retrieval – It is used to retrieve data from the database on the basis of need. Because once the data is entered, in the future mostly the user only needs some of the selected records, the process of finding those selected records are called queries, performing them is an important task of the database management system, it will further explain in the database language. It can be understood from this because a normal user is not concerned with the complexity of the database .it is the primary duty of and DBMS-based application program to provide a gentle interface from which users can retrieve required data from the database.

iv. Data Administrator – It is used to register and monitor users and it is used for maintaining data integrity, providing data security, monitoring performance, and concurrency control. A database administrator is a person who monitors and controls the software of database management.

Most of such tasks are performed automatically by DBMS software, but in some places, human is also required. There are some decisions that cannot be taken by the program. Database administration is required in those situations; this is done because many times the data is real data in that the dependency on the program alone is not correct. Therefore a responsible person is also required on whom the responsibility of this entire database management system software can be given. Because sometimes there are situations in which the reasoning ability of man is required. Which cannot be done by a normal database management system?

Monitoring, controlling, changing the DBMS software, all the decision-making work is done by the database administrator only.

5.4 Components of DBMS

There are mainly two basic components of DBMS .Data description module and data manipulation module.

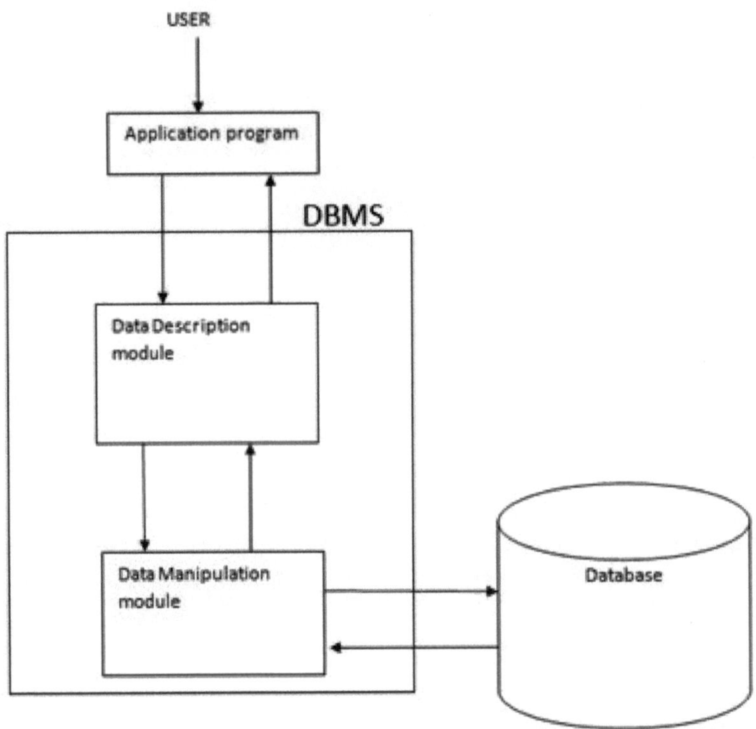

Fig: component of DBMS

First of all, users interact with any application program that provides an interface to access the database Application program request to DBMS for appropriate action on behalf of the user. The data description module analyzes the data requirements of an application program and transfers control to the data manipulation module. Then data manipulation module accesses the required data from the database.

We can understand this with the help of an example. Suppose there is a student database with fields of roll number, name, father name, address, subject marks, class, and semester. And a user wants to know the percentage of a particular student. So its requests any application program that is based on DBMS. And application program requests to DBMS.

The data description module analyzes the exact requirement of data. There is no need for a student's father's name, address, class, or semester to know the percentage of marks. Only roll number, name, and subject marks fields are required to calculate the percentage of marks. So data description modules filter the request and then pass it to the data manipulation module for only three fields of the student database. Data manipulation module searches the record for a given roll number and retrieves fields that are defined by the data description module.

5.5 Elements of DBMS

The following are the elements of a database management system:-

- Hardware
- Software
- Data
- Users
- Procedures

Hardware

Our computer system is the main one in the hardware which is used to store and access our database. This refers to physical electronic devices such as computers, I/O storage devices, etc. come. Hard disk is mostly used to store data in computer systems.

Hardware mainly includes storage devices (hard disk, pen drive, flash memory, CD, DVD) for DBMS operations. Hardware is the physical element of DBMS because ultimately data is stored physically. It is like a root of DBMS.

Software

Software is a basic component of DBMS. It is a group of programs that are used to control and manage the entire database. Under this DBMS software, operating system, and application programs come.

DBMS software is an interface between users and the database. It provides a very easy interface through which the data in the database is stored, updated, and retrieved. The overall structure of DBMS is based on this element.

Data

Data is the soul component of DBMS. DBMS collects stores, processes, and accesses data. The actual data, operational data, and metadata are stored in the database. Without data, we cannot imagine DBMS. Each and every operation on DBMS is only and only for data.

Users

There are many types of users who access the data according to their needs. The capability and needs of each user are different. Basically, the overall DBMS is made for users. Database administrator, Database designers, End-users and Application programmers are some common DBMS users.

Procedures

Procedures contain the rules and instructions for using the database management system. A procedure describes how to use the database in the system. Such as: - Installing and setting up DBMS, logging in to the database, logout, backing up the database, and handling the database, etc. The efficiency of any DBMS program is based on how effective a procedure is defined.

5.6 Properties of DBMS

Any DBMS must support four basic properties. In short, it is known as ACID properties.

A is for Atomicity: either a transaction is fully completed or not started. This means the partial transaction is not allowed in DBMS. For example, A gives 100 rs. To B. To complete this transaction A account is debited with hundred rupees and B account is credited with hundred rupees. Both operations are mandatory to perform to complete the transaction. If one of the two operations does not perform, then the principle of atomicity states that no operation should be performed. The meaning is clear that it cannot happen that money is deducted from one account and money is not deposited in the other's account.

C is for Consistency: database is consistent before and after the transaction. It refers to the correctness of a database. There are many such situations in the database, to complete a transaction, many different operations have to be filled in the form, such as the second operation should be performed only after the first operation or the output that will come after the first and second operations, the third operation Will depend on the same output means that we can say that the transactions of the database depend on each other. So even after the transaction is completed, the DBMS checks what is the difference between the post-transactional state and the previous state? And what the user wanted; overall, the final result would have been verified instead of intermediate.

I is for Isolation: When there is more than one transaction, sometimes a situation arises that one transaction can have an effect on another transaction, so the database management system avoids this type of situation. For example, if two transactions access a common memory area, then when one transaction accesses its common memory area, then the other transaction should wait, this condition is followed by the DBMS otherwise it can create a serious problem.

D is for Durability It means to maintain the state of the database. if a transaction is completed then DBMS maintains the state after the end of the transaction. In any case, that state should not be changed even if the system fails. Many times it happens that after a system failure, the system resets itself, in that case, if the transaction is reset then there can be a loss.

5.7 Characteristics of DBMS

No data redundancy At the time of design of the system, special care is taken that there should be no duplication of data because in the database management system, the data is also kept in the format of tables, in this way the database is divided into rows and columns and it connects to other tables as well, thus reducing the chances of duplication of data

Data Consistency Data consistency means that the data is stored in the database correctly at any cost. Since the database management system works within the operating system itself and the operating system executes multiprogramming or multiple programs simultaneously, then there is a possibility that the database will be corrupted or due to any reason, the operating system can access the database. So DBMS Take care of this thing that such a mistake should not happen.

Multi-user DBMS support multiuser features. It means that through the database system, many users can access the database at the same time. Sometimes our data is not stored on one system but is stored on many different systems and the users accessing those systems are also different, so having a multi-user facility makes the execution of the database faster because, In this, all the users can access the DBMS simultaneously, as well as the consistency of the data is also maintained.

Security means maintaining the privacy integrity and availability of the data. Privacy means only authorized users can read the data and integrity means only authorized persons can change the data and availability means whenever a user wants to access data he can. Due to any reason if the system cannot provide the data at the time of user requirement it is not a good sign of the system. And DBMS provide all these three fundamental elements of security

5.8 Types of DBMS / Database model

If the user inputs data, then in what order should we store that data? Either you can arrange it directly in the format of an array or can store it in the forms of the matrix. But while storing the data, we have to prepare this model to be easily found in the future, so different models are made. There can be many ways to store data.

It is mainly of 4 types. Which is as follows:-

i. Hierarchical

ii. Relational

iii. Network

iv. Object-oriented

i Hierarchical model

In this model, the data is stored in the format of a tree. That is to say, the order to store the data is like a tree. In this model, there is a root and there are branches. It is also called the parent-child relationship model. Which one parent has many children and then the same child becomes the parent. It also has children, in the same way; data is stored in this model as well.

In this database, the data is arranged in a tree structure. That is, the data is stored in a top-down or bottom-up format. There is a parent-child relationship in the data.

This model has a parent-child relationship. In this model, each entity has only one parent and many children. In this model, there is only one entity which we call root.

To access any data in this model, we have to traverse each tree until the record is found. This is more useful for those places where the data is already placed in some order (ascending and descending).

In this, the searching of data starts from the root node. That route has two children. One child is selected. Then it becomes a child-parent model. Similarly, this sequence continues until the desired data is found.

Most of this database is used in the banking and telecommunication fields.

Its main advantage is that in this we can access and update the data very fast.

Its disadvantage is that its structure cannot be applied to everyone. Of course, it is not flexible.

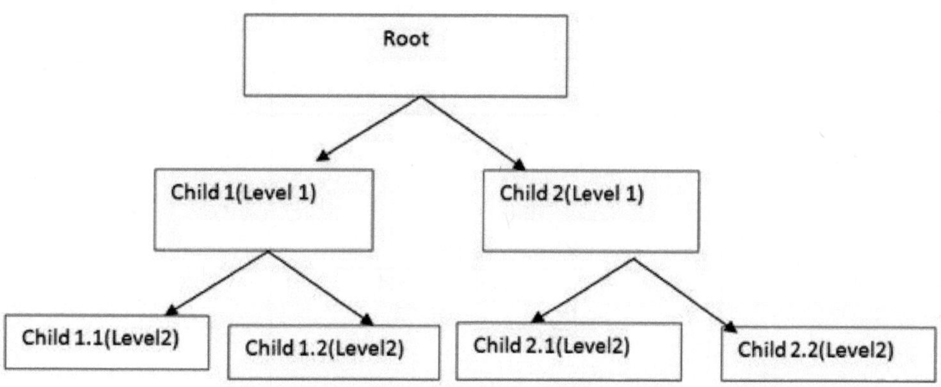

Fig: Hierarchical data model

Example:

We can understand the concept of the Hierarchical data model with an example. Suppose we are working in a world database where information related to every country is kept. After that database is created, separate databases should be created for different countries, in which each database will display information about one country. After some time a separate database should be made for each country for the information of different states, similarly, after some time a separate database should be made for each state in which the information of their districts should be created.

That is, the names of many countries in the database of the whole world, then in the second database, separate databases should be created for different countries. That is, there will be a country field in the world's database, followed by a state field in the country's database, followed by a city field in the state's database.

Hence this type of database is called a hierarchical data model where the fields of one database become the new database later on. It is very easy to find any information in this data model and this thing works very fast. Suppose someone needs any information about Varanasi city of Uttar Pradesh of India. First of all, get one information from India field from world database then will use a database containing only India. After that, in the table containing India, the table of Uttar Pradesh will be directly selected. After this, only the Varanasi district will be selected from the state table.

Thus we see that in this model we do not need to access unnecessary fields. If all the data was in one table, then you can imagine how much searching would have to be done to search only Varanasi.

World

Sr. no.	Country	Field 1	Field 2	..	..
1	America	-	-	-	-
2	India	-	-	-	-
3	China	-	-	-	-
.	-	-	-	-	-
.	-	-	-	-	-
.	-	-	-	-	-

India

Sr. no.	State	Field 1	Field 2	..	..
1	UP	-	-	-	-
2	MP	-	-	-	-
3	HP	-	-	-	-
.	-	-	-	-	-
.	-	-	-	-	-
.	-	-	-	-	-

Uttar Pradesh

Sr. no.	City	Field 1	Field 2	..	..
1	Varanasi	-	-	-	-
2	Kanpur	-	-	-	-
3	Prayagraj	-	-	-	-
.	-	-	-	-	-
.	-	-	-	-	-
.	-	-	-	-	-

In this example world is root database, India is a child database for world database (Level 1) 1 and Uttar Pradesh is child database of India database (Level 2).

Note: In the dictionary, English words are also stored under Hierarchical data model.

ii Relational model

It is also known as RDBMS (Relational Database Management System).

In relational database model data is stored in the form of tables. It is mainly a collection of several types of tables. In a relational database management system, many tables are interconnected.

In this type of database model data are stored in many e related tables. The basic entity of this database model is a table. DBMS is a collection of many related files and RDBMS is a collection of many related databases. A single table represents a single entity. For a separate entity, a separate table is created.

The table is a collection of rows and columns. Row represent records of a particular field and column represent the field .in the term of RDBMS column represents the attribute of an entity. in RDBMS table is known as an entity and the column of the table is called attributes and the row of the table is the value of an attribute.

There are many tables in RDBMS which are related to each other with the help of key (specific and unique value field), their existence is also different and they can also be used together if needed. Suppose a single student sits in the exam as well as he is also related to some sport, then a separate table is made for the exam, a separate table is made for the sport. The student is the same, so he will also be related to the exam table and will also be related to the sport table. If one wants complete information about that student, some of it will be found from the table containing the exam and some will also be found from the table containing the sport. Similarly, students can be related to any other table.

So we can say that RDBMS is a form of data collection where we can store our data in a form of many rows and columns. Where the columns are predefined and the value of rows is to be inserted by the user.

We can understand the concept with an example.

Table 1 :STUDENT BASIC RECORDS						
SR. NO.	ROLL NUMBER	NAME	FATHER'S NAME	DATE OF BIRTH	CITY	MOB.
1	21108001	AJAY KUMAR	NEELKANTH KUMAR	12/5/2001	VARANASI	-
2	21108002	VIKAS YADAV	RAMASHISH YADAV	27/12/2000	PRAYAGRAJ	-
3	21108003	SUNEL SINGH	DEV NARAYAN SINGH	1/5/1999	VARANASI	-
4	21108004	MOH. ABDUL KHAN	NUR ABDUL	8/8/2002	BALLIA	-
5	21108005	KISHOR AWASHTI	RAJSHEKHAR AWASTHI	12/1/2001	AZAMGARH	-
6	21108006	ACHINTYA SINGHAL	BRIJMOHAN SINGHAL	29/09/2000	KANPUR	-
7	21108007	SHREYA GUPTA	KRISHNA GUPTA	28/05/2002	JAUNPUR	-
8	21108008	KESHAW PANDEY	DEEPAK PANDEY	3/6/2000	GAZIABAD	-
9	21108009	ROHAN VERMA	KAILASH VERMA	31/12/2002	VARANASI	-

Table2:STUDENT CURRENT RECORD					
SR. NO.	ROLL NUMBER	CURRENT YEAR	SUBJECT STREAM	PREVIOUS RESULT	
1	21108001	FIRST YEAR	COMMERCE	PASSED	
2	21108002	FIRST YEAR	COMMERCE	PASSED	
3	21108003	FIRST YEAR	COMMERCE	PASSED	
4	21108004	FIRST YEAR	COMMERCE	PASSED	
5	21108005	FIRST YEAR	COMMERCE	PASSED	
6	21108006	FIRST YEAR	COMMERCE	PASSED	
7	21108007	FIRST YEAR	COMMERCE	PASSED	
8	21108008	FIRST YEAR	COMMERCE	PASSED	
9	21108009	FIRST YEAR	COMMERCE	PASSED	

Table3:STUDENT QUALIFYING EXAM RECORD					
SR. NO.	ROLL NUMBER	QUALIFYING EXAM	SUBJECT STREAM	MARKS OBTAINED	TOTAL MARKS
1	21108001	10+2	COMMERCE	410	500
2	21108002	10+2	COMMERCE	425	500
3	21108003	10+2	COMMERCE	450	500
4	21108004	10+2	SCIENCE	880	1000
5	21108005	10+2	COMMERCE	390	500
6	21108006	10+2	COMMERCE	389	500
7	21108007	10+2	SCIENCE	890	1000
8	21108008	10+2	COMMERCE	405	500
9	21108009	10+2	COMMERCE	419	500

Here are 3 tables. Table 1 Student Basic Record, Table 2 Student Current Record, and Table 3 Student Qualifying Exam Record. DBMS is an example as there are 3 different tables and they are also related to each other by roll number (key). One table has a relation to other tables so it is an example of a relational database.

Table name = entity Student Basic Record is an entity, Student Current Record is an entity and Student Qualifying Exam Record is also an entity.

Fields (column) of table are known as attributes of entity.

SR. NO., ROLL NUMBER, NAME, FATHER'S NAME, DATE OF BIRTH, CITY, MOB. Are attributes of table 1 entity.

SR. NO., ROLL NUMBER, CURRENT YEAR, SUBJECT STREAM, PREVIOUS RESULT are attributes of table 2 entity.

SR. NO. ,ROLL NUMBER, QUALIFYING EXAM,SUBJECT STREAM,MARKS OBTAINED,TOTAL MARKS are attributes of table 3 entity.

All the rows (records) of the table are known as values of attributes.

The existences of all the three tables are different though they are one. If a user needs any information related to student basic record then DBMS will provide that information only from Table 1 like if someone wants to ask the date of birth of roll number 21108001 then this information will be available from Table 1 only Or if you want to know the current year of that student, then this information will be available only from Table 2. Similarly, if any information is needed to be related to the qualifying exam of the student, then this information can be obtained from Table 3 itself.

That is to say, having separate existence of all three tables, different information related to them can be easily obtained. But this is just an example of a database management system. In a relational database management system, we can also get such information which can be obtained by combining these three tables. Like if we have to see which stream Ajay Kumar belonged to and in which year he is currently studying. Ajay Kumar's name information is only in table 1 because only the student's name is in table1. Ajay Kumar's name will be searched from table 1 and his roll number will be obtained then that roll number will be found in table 2 that in which year he is and the same roll number will be checked from table 3 that what is his stream?

In this way, this is the biggest advantage of a relational database management system that we can get any information by keeping the data separately and also by mixing them together. In our given example, only roll number is common in all three tables. Name of any student, father's name, date of birth is not being used again and again. It is only in table1 but if a user wants all the information of a student then instead of creating a new table from these three tables all the different information can be collected in one place and provided to the user. The user is never able to know that all this information is getting from one table or is stored in different tables; this is the main advantage of a relational database management system.

Advantages of RDBMS

The most important advantage of relational databases is that they enable users to easily categorize and store data that can be queried and filtered to extract specific information in the future. Extending relational databases is much easier than other databases and does not depend on physical organization. After the original database creation, a new field can be easily added without modifying all existing applications.

Accuracy: Data is stored only once, thus eliminating data duplication meaning that the same data does not have to be stored again and again. Due to which the chances of making a mistake are greatly reduced.

Flexibility: It is easy for the users to solve even the most complex queries as the databases are stored separately and in a very organized manner.

Multi user support system: Multiple users can access the same database. Means many users can access the same database at the same time. This saves a lot of time. And the performance of the system increases.

Security: Data in different tables within an RDBMS can be limited to allow access only by authorized users. The chance of loss of data due to any reason is very less. Sometimes there is a possibility of a loss of data due to many reasons. RDBMS has to be managed on its own. In this way our data is very secure in RDBMS.

iii Network model

This database uses the network structure to create relationships between entities.

It is used in very large databases where more data is collected than usual. This database also works like hierarchical but a child can have many parents in it. In this, the child is called the member and the parents are called the occupier.

In this database model the entities are arranged or displayed in a graph so that they can be easily accessed from many paths. The biggest problem with hierarchical models was that a child has only one parent, that is, there is only one way to reach a child. Therefore, data searching takes more time than having only one path. And if for some reason that one path also ends, then it will be impossible to search that child (data).

Therefore, its main advantage is that in this we can access the data easily and securely and its design is also easy.

Its disadvantage is that updating and inserting records is very complex.

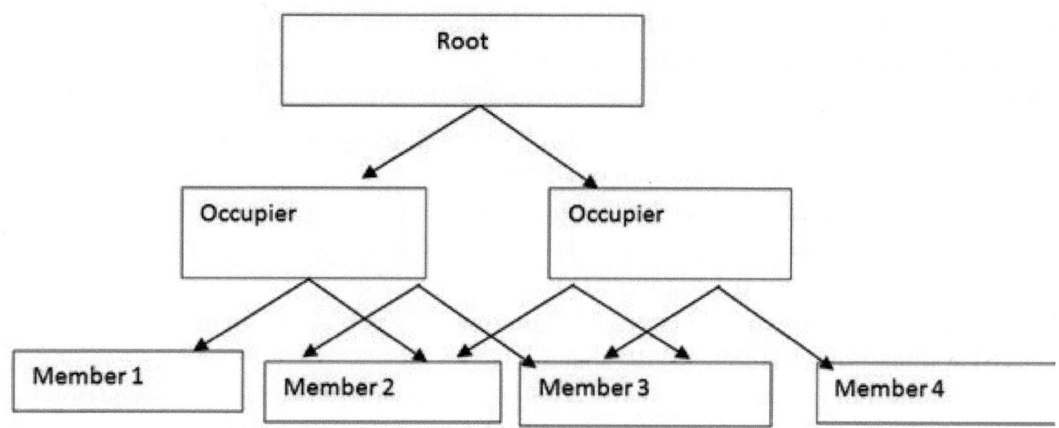

Fig: network model of DBMS

We can see from figure that there are many ways to reach any specific member.

Features of the network model:

The following are some of the most salient features of the network model -

It is similar to the hierarchical model but can represent redundancy or duplicity of data more efficiently than the hierarchical model.

There may be one or more paths from the previous node to the successor node/s.

A linked list (circular) structure is used to operate the network model. Where one program holds the current position data and another program navigates from record to record by following the relationships in which the record participates.

Advantages

> It is very fast and quick data access.

> Complex queries can be created very easily.

> Chances of data loss are very less.

> There are multiple paths to reach a single data.

> The reliability of DBMS increases.

Disadvantages

> A user must be very familiar with the structure of the database to work through the set structures.

> The same person can access the database properly who has good knowledge about the internal structure of the database.

> Updating this type of database is a very complex task. No set structure can change without affecting the application program that uses this structure to navigate through the data. If you change the structure of any one set, you must also modify all references to that structure from within the application program.

> Due to the network model, there are many ways to reach the member, due to this, sometimes a collision situation also arises due to which the situation of network jam is created, and the whole system becomes slow.

iv Object-oriented model

In this model data is stored in the form of objects. And its structure is called class. It provides programming capability. In this, less code are needed to create a database application. And maintaining the codes is also very easy.

These databases support most of the programming languages:- Like:- c++, JAVA, RUBY, PYTHON, etc.

Its main advantage is that it is very easy to maintain.

Its disadvantage is that it does not have its own query language like relational sql.

Exercises

Objective type question

Choose the correct answer for the followings.

1. DBMS is stand for

(a) Database management system (b) directory based memory system

(c) Disk based memory system (d) none of these

2. DBMS is a

(a) Driver software (b) networking device (c) software (d) printing device

3. Which of the following is not a function of DBMS?

(a) Data storage (b) data printing (c) data updating (d) data retrieval

4. ----------- is a property that described various characteristics of an entity in DBMS

(a) Attributes (b) relationship (c) column (d) row

5. The creation of a database and its tables is a function of which component of the database system

(a)Users (b) application (c) DBMS (d) database

6. Data redundancy and inconsistency is the challenge in which of the following system

(a) Traditional file system (b) DBMS (c)RDBMS (d) none of these

7. -------------- is used to define the overall design of the database.

(a)Schema (b) application program (c) DDL (d) DML

8. Means multiple copies of the same data item.

(a) Data reduction (b) Data integrity (c) Data redundancy (d) Data consistency

9. Which of the following is not a function of database administrator?

(a) Network maintenance (b) routine maintenance

(c) Schema definition (d) authorization of data access

10. Which of the following is a data model?

(a) Hierarchical (b) network (c)relational (d)all of these

Theoretical questions

1. What do you mean by DBMS? Explain the basic concept of DBMS.

2. What are the main advantages of DBMS?

3. List some characteristics of DBMS.

4. Differentiate between hierarchical and network database models with suitable diagrams.

5. Explain different types of DBMS.

6. Write in detail about the ACID properties of DBMS.

7. Demonstrate the concept of the relational database model.

8. Using implementing the concept RDBMS design a database model for railways system.

9. What do you understand by object-oriented database model?

CHAPTER SIX

USES OF DBMS

In this chapter, we are going to know the relevance of the data management systems and the interpretation of DBMS applications.

6.1 Relevance of DBMS

DBMS is used in various areas due to its unmatchable advantages. The utility and relevance of database management systems today are in almost every field. Be it the field of teaching, the field of research class or the industrial sector, or the business sector. Due to the features of the database management system, it is used in every field today and every sector benefits a lot from it. The basic objective of every organization is to make maximum development and decision making is the biggest contributor to development. Unless an organization takes the right decision at the right time, it cannot progress. If an organization or person does not take the right decision at the right time, then its development gets affected. Even if the decision is taken late, it is not effective, and then it is very important for the decision to be correct and to be taken at the right time. Most of the decision management work is done by the person in an organization, but the person has his own capabilities, he cannot take decisions faster than the computer and also cannot store much information as compared to the computer. Therefore, the computer is required for development in an institution, but we know that a computer alone is not capable of doing any work, it can work only with the help of software. Before database management system software, work was done on the file system, he used to use the computer but he could not make maximum use. We should not forget that one of the fundamental purposes of software or program is that they can make maximum use of available hardware. . Optimum Utilization is the main objective of any organization and management. That management system is considered good which is capable of producing maximum output from the available resources. Suppose in an industrial unit, a machine produces 100 units in a day and if more than 100 units are produced from the same machine at the same time using some other method, then the other system will be considered more useful. For this reason, the relevance of computer programs or any software remains in every field even today because the development of hardware requires more money, as well as the cost of its maintenance, is also high. And the cost has an important place in any organization, especially in the business line, because if the cost of an item increases, then its value will also increase and an increase in the price can affect its sales. Because of this cost becomes an important topic in every business. And this is the reason that no organization changes the hardware again and again. For this reason, the field of computer science developed because the software provides the ability to make maximum use of available resources, in this sequence many types of software were also developed gradually.

Earlier traditional methods were used to store data. At the same time, there were no very powerful tools be available for data processing. With the advent of database management, there was a radical change in the data processing. Available data was used more and more effectively.

No additional equipment is required to use DBMS. Nowadays database management system is developing even more and has reached many new technologies. It is also used in Big Data. The basic reason behind designing database management system software was to reduce the cost of the commodity in any organization, especially in industrial units. It is because of DBMS that any business organization can take effective decisions and we know how effective DBMS is in taking effective decisions due to its various features.

In today's modern society, along with computers, technology has developed a lot in many other areas as well. Today computer is also available in its different advanced form. The computer has reduced to a mobile form, the speed of the Internet has become very fast, the computational power of the processor has become much faster than before, the memory is also more available, the speed of the supercomputer should be thousands of times faster. It's over. But all this is dependent on the software somewhere and that particular software is the Data Base Management System. As we know that any device, no matter how much any organization develops, all have the same basic objective and that is decision management. The organization develops because of taking the right decisions at the right time. And the most important contribution in decision making is how we analyze the available information. The ability to analyze the information as good as that found in database management system software is not found in any other.

DBMS was designed to solve basic problems related to storage, management, access, security, and auditing of data in traditional file systems.

Traditional database applications were developed on top of databases, which faced challenges such as data redundancy, isolation, lack of integrity, and difficulty managing data access. A layer of abstraction was needed at the physical and logical level between the users or the apps and the database.

We can understand the relevance of database management system software through the following points:

Independence and abstraction of the database management system keep the complexities of the system away from the user. The user never knows where and how his data is being stored. Organizations can change the physical schema of a database system without requiring changes to the logical schema that governs database relationships. As a result, organizations can upgrade storage and scale up infrastructure without affecting database operations. Similarly, changes to the logical schema can be applied without making changes to the apps and services that access the database.

Data security The most prominent feature of a database management system is the security system it provides. DBMS allows organizations to implement policies that enable compliance and security. The databases are available to the appropriate users according to organizational policies. The DBMS system is also responsible for maintaining optimum performance of query operations while ensuring the validity, security, and consistency of the updated data items in the database.

Data sharing once the data is stored in the DBMS, it can be accessed by many people in many places. So that it provide fast and efficient collaboration between users.

Data access and auditing Controlled access to the database. Logging-related access activities allow organizations to be audited for security and compliance.

Data integration The existing database management system controls redundancy, due to which data is stored in one place. Database management systems also use the same common space to handle many types of queries. A single interface is used to manage a database with logical and physical relationships.

Uniform Management and Administration A single console interface for performing basic administrative tasks simplifies the task for database administrators and IT users.

For data-driven business organizations, DBMS can turn into extremely complex technology solutions, which may require dedicated resources and internal expertise. The size, cost, and performance of DBMS vary with system architecture and use cases, and should therefore be evaluated accordingly. Furthermore, a DBMS failure can cause significant damage to organizations that fail to maintain the optimum functionality of the DBMS system.

6.2 Advantages of Database Management System

To understand the concept of relevance of DBMS better we need to know the benefits of DBMS. Unlike file based data management system, DBMS has many benefits. We are highlighting some of the important benefits here-

Simplicity

DBMS allows us to understand the data better from a clear and simple logical point of view. With DBMS, it is easy to implement multiple operations like delete, insert or create file or data.

Data Integrity

Data integrity means that the data is consistent and accurate in the database. This is necessary because a DBMS consists of multiple databases. All these databases contain data that is visible to many users. Therefore, it is essential to ensure that the data is consistent and correct across all databases for all users.

Data Security

Data security is an important concept in databases. Only authorized users should be allowed to access the database and their identity should be authenticated using username and password. Unauthorized users should not be allowed to access the database under any circumstances as it violates the integrity constraints.

A DBMS provides a better platform for data privacy thereby helping companies to provide better data security.

More Data Integration

Due to the database management system, we have well-managed and synchronous access to the data, making it easy to handle. It also gives an integrated view of how a particular organization is operating and keeps track of how one segment of the company affects another segment.

Lack of Data Inconsistency

Data inconsistency between files occurs when different versions of the same data appear in different places. Data consistency is ensured in the database; there is no data redundancy. In addition, any database changes are reflected immediately by all users, and there is no data inconsistency.

Fast Data Access

The database management system helps users to quickly answer questions such as:

How much bonus has been given to the employees in the last two years?

How many customers return their products in the last two months?

What is the profit of the previous year?

In which year has the maximum profit been made in the last ten years?

Making Better Decisions

The impact of the decision taken by the management on the sales of the product can also be traced.

Due to DBMS, we have now improved and managed the data access due to which we can generate better quality information leading to better decision making.

Better quality ultimately improves validity, accuracy and time taken to read the data. It does not guarantee data quality; It provides a framework to make it easy to enhance data quality.

Recovery and Backup

The DBMS automatically takes care of the recovery and backup. Users do not need to take periodic backups as this is taken care of by the DBMS. In addition, it also restores the database to its previous state after a system failure or crash.

Increase in End User Productivity

Available data is converted into useful information with the help of a combination of tools. It helps end users to make smart, informative and quick decisions that can make the difference between success and failure in the global economy.

Additionally, today DBMS is also serving as the backbone of many advanced technology practices such as BigData, Data Science, Data Modeling and Machine Learning.

6.3 Interpretations of DBMS Application

There are many advantages of DBMS. Keeping this in mind it is used in many organizations, every organization has different requirements. Different organizations have different objectives in different areas and each organization makes different types of plans to achieve its objective. Every organization takes different types of decisions keeping in mind its objective such as recruitment of employees, purchase and sale of movable and immovable property, budget management, appointment to higher positions and development of quality of work system etc.

We can mainly understand the use of DBMS application by dividing it into two areas

Education

Industry

Field of education

Although the field of education is very wide, all the work related to the field of education has a basic objective and that is to spread knowledge. It is not that this area is completely different from all other areas; many works are also done here. Improving quality is also the ultimate aim of the education sector and DBMS software has always proved to be a powerful weapon for quality development. Following are some of the major areas of education.

University

The activities of the University are of international standard. Hence, the storage of information here is excessive as the students coming to the university are of different age groups in different languages from different countries, thus there is a lot of diversity among them. The role becomes very important because if the data here is not handled properly then carrying out various types of non-academic activities will become a very complex task for the university because the aim of the university is to provide advanced education but at the same time to award degrees to its students. If the university's data management is not done properly, there may be a disparity in degrees on one hand, and on the other hand, the credibility of the university is also affected because if any mistake is found in the data management of a university, then it will also affect the reputation of the university. Nowadays the picture of universities has changed a lot through the internet. Today students can get an education from the university even by staying away. Today, thanks to the Internet, it is possible to enroll study, take exams, and even obtain degrees remotely, without having to physically go to universities. In such a situation, it can be easily understood that what is the importance of software like Database Management System in any university? Management of data on such a large scale is possible only with software like DBMS.

College

While on the one hand, universities provide education to students from all over the world, on the other hand, they also provide recognition to many colleges. You must have heard many times that a college is affiliated with a university, so the college always has a relationship with the university because the college itself is not capable of awarding degrees, it only provides education. From the enrollment of the student to his examination, his mark sheet, his degree, etc., all the work is done by the university itself, but the college works in an intermediary manner, even in these circumstances, the database management system has an important contribution. Because where the college has to store the student data on one side, on the other hand, it has to be processed and sent to the university and then the information provided by the university has to be provided back to the students, in this way the data is collected at the college level here. The movement is very high, keeping this type of activity in mind; database management system software has a very important place at the college level.

School

Compared to university and college, the level of the school is much less in terms of geographical area or in terms of numbers, but the students studying here are future generations, so at this level, the quality of such an institution is the main focus because even here Data has to be managed and the management of data is directly related to the students. School students are less than college or university students in age, so anything has a deep impact on them, so any data in any of their data has to be managed. In case of any type of mistake, it assumes the fault of the whole system, so the management of data here must be quality-oriented, so also the database management system software has a serious place here. Although many small schools ignore this and do all the work either manually or with any normal application software but the institutes or schools which use DBMS to manage the data is definitely a quality it has a direct impact on the student's education, in fact, due to the software, the publication of results can be possible on time, and it is obvious that if the examination is taken on time. if you get the result on time, it saves a lot of time, here the time is directly related to the students.

Because if a student's time is wasted, then in a way it destroys the future fate of the country. Prior to DBMS software, there was often a problem of sessions late at the university, college, or school level, and the main reason for this was also the lack of data management, so many students have enrolled so many students that it took a long time to process their data It would take Due to the software in DBMS, this time is saved and the session gets improved. That's why we can say that DBMS software is also very useful in the world of education.

Other Education Fields

Apart from the University College or school, there are many such organizations or areas where teaching-related work is done such as coaching institute, training institute, training academy, even here DBMS software is as useful as in University College or school. Because basically, the task of database management software is the management of data, if the movement of data in an institution is high or happens frequently, there is a need for a powerful tool to manage the data and the institutions about which are here now. It has been talked about there too often in every new session new students come and old ones leave, thus the movement of data happens here very quickly, hence the usefulness of database management system is relevant here.

Examination commission

The main function of various types of commissions related to the examination like Staff Selection Commission or Public Service Commission etc. is to conduct the examination. The commission has to appoint the selected students to different types of posts. In such a situation, the usefulness of the database management system becomes even more relevant because here the database is related to one's life, Staff Selection Commission, Public Service Commission, Railway related board or bank or any institute which conducts the examination and if its If the result is related to their future, then any data related to the examination is much more valuable than the normal data, any kind of error in it, any kind of mistake, any error cannot be accepted. An error here means one's real life has to be affected, in such a way, DBMS software proves to be a boon in a way. Before DBMS software, it used to take a lot of time to conduct the examination by the commission, due to which the appointment on the posts took time. The work was affected and eventually, it had an impact on the development of the whole country, thus the database management system indirectly contributes significantly to the development of the country.

In industry

The world of data is constantly changing and growing every moment. This in turn has created infinite new dimensions of growth and challenges companies across the world. By accurately recording the data, updating and tracking themes on an efficient and regular basis, the company can address its challenges on one hand and, on the other, tap the immense potential of this sector.

By collecting minute and updated data, companies are using the said information to systematically achieve their goals on the one hand and strategically strengthen their business on the other. Some of the activities that follow the collection of data include creating accounting reports, calculating sales estimates, and generating customer invoices. This data and its insights are then made available to the organization's management and employees through a computerized database. One of the proven ways to manage the relationships between different database elements is through the use of database management systems, which are an integral part of the functioning of companies and organizations around the world today.

Therefore, database management systems are important and important links in data creation as well as management. These are essential for the effective handling and management of data. It also helps companies to move said data through the entire system.

Some of the reasons why data management systems are important include the following:

For data access within the organization

Modern database management systems rely on a programming language called Structured Query Language. This language is used to access, update and delete data in its tables. Database systems also include programs that include Microsoft's SQL Server and open-source MySQL Query that enable external programs to access their data through SQL queries. For example, a web page may display information or data that includes product data and descriptions, photos, and prices. This information is readily available to the user when the web server software is connected to the relational database management system.

Maintain a strong connection between the two data table

One of the most important functions of a relational database management system program is that it allows different data tables to be related to each other. When a database contains information about employee data on sales of their product in one table and sales employee data in another table, a relational approach is needed to manage their relationships in an organized and simple style. This system in turn can help managers understand important statistics such as which seller is able to sell the most or which product is being sold by a particular seller.

Improved Update Process

A useful and productive database management system not only allows brand managers to enter new information, but also to update existing information and delete information they no longer need. For example, when a seller is able to sell a few units of a product, the person can enter the transaction information into the relational management system including certain details such as the person's name, the product containing the customer information, and the number of products. Number sold by him. The relational database management system will record new records and update all necessary information, enabling brands to effectively track and sell their products.

Data in a better way

Relational database management systems allow brand managers to maintain and build on their data for years in a row. The various tables in a relational database management system allow brand managers to search throughout their systems for specific information. The company manager can easily access any information he needs by using a particular parameter. It is also available to customers who can search for a range of features including price, color, and brand. By storing information in a predictable and sequential format, it enables users to get the information they need.

With so much information available to companies, it is important for brands of all sectors and groups to invest in a database management system. Today almost all companies and brands run on database systems. These organized stores of information can help brands store all kinds of information which they can not only sort but make available at the click of a mouse. In short, database management systems help brands track every part of their business faster, more effectively, efficiently, and successfully than ever before.

In market research

Reduce the amount of paper you need to store. Manage large volumes of long-term survey results, compare survey results across years from the same customer, similar criteria easily, quickly, and effectively. Surveys are always updated quickly, avoiding duplication, avoiding missing information (software warns when insufficient information is needed), information divergence (causing re-entering from paper to file), or data (papers). Because of the loss Removed immediately Control of enumerators and accuracy of survey results is simple. The initial cost may increase; however, the long-term development cost will be reduced.

In sales management

Allow to manage millions of customers at the same time, and store each customer's entire transaction. Find one or multiple customers with the required attribute. The marketing department may store information about the strategy and the customer allows the sales department to edit basic information, customer service information, and orders. Production and warehouse department store production results and warehouse status information. The accounting department stores order transactions and accrued costs.

Integrating, storing, and integrating personal data of the above departments, from finding sales, invoicing, and transaction history, providing information to clarify, creating customer service strategy (based on transaction history), reducing the percentage of customer duplication is done.

Review of history data, comparison of data over the years also helps the company in approximating the position of revenue as per the time, environmental conditions, etc.

In human resource management

HR is a process that runs from pre-recruitment planning to the departure of personnel. Everyone has different information, which is difficult to manage by different file papers, especially when updating, changing private information, data "matching" is not uncommon. Appropriate software will help leaders:

Personnel information is stored synchronously throughout the process before, during, and after working in the company: basic information about personnel, performance appraisal results, salary, reward, discipline, promotion... HR information software helps organize and manage the personal information of personnel during the process of working in an enterprise.

The reporting system will help in the comprehensive evaluation, leading to the formulation of effective training, recruitment plans.

In small business

Small businesses run on databases. These stores of organized information can store almost every type of data, and they can sort that information and deliver it to you with a click of the mouse. Business databases help small-business owners organize and track their customers, inventory, and employees.

Customer Relationship Management (CRM)

A customer relationship management (CRM) database can help a small business manage its business -- the lifeline of its customers. A CRM database organizes all the information a company has about its accounts, contacts, leads, and opportunities. A single customer's record may include his contact details, the date and amount of his last order, the total amount of his purchases for the previous year, a list of products and products returned by him, details of customer service calls, and more. The database can also be used to manage marketing and promotions, export email addresses, and generate shipping labels.

Inventory Tracking Database

An inventory tracking database can tell a retail business how much inventory is in a warehouse, in a storage room, and on store shelves. Integrated bar codes and scanners form a complete tracking system, monitoring products as they move from location to location and updating the database so you don't have to count inventory in the warehouse. A database can also alert you when products and supplies are running low so you can order more before you run out of essentials.

Payroll and Scheduling Database

Using a database to manage employee information can make scheduling easier and help prevent payroll errors. An employee database contains fields such as hourly wage, salary or commission, tax withholding rate, year-to-date earnings, and earned vacation time. Other employee benefits, such as health insurance and retirement account contributions, may also be entered into the database. Two or more databases can be combined to create a relationship between sales reports in the personnel database and the accounts they are responsible for in the CRM database.

Business data analysis

The robust reporting features of databases make them useful resources for analyzing data and predicting future trends. For example, a productivity report might show that productivity slows so much on the Friday afternoon before a three-day holiday weekend that you can allow employees to leave early on those days. A sales promotion effectiveness report may show that sales of some products increased after an email promotion while sales of other products increased after an in-store promotion. Customer behavior is predictable, and a database can help you anticipate and meet your customers' expectations.

6.4 Application of DBMS

Banking

Banking is a major sector where data flow is very frequent. The banking sector is a very essential place for DBMS application. DBMS application is used to maintain customer information, account activities and account details, payment transaction details, deposit transaction details, loan-related data, etc in the bank.

HR management

Human resources are the heart of any organization. Basically, every wish of any company or organization is taken by human beings. Hence HR (Employee) records are very important to maintain. DBMS is used in human resource management to maintain information about employees, salary, payroll, deductions, production per annum, checks, etc.

sales

If an organization is based on sailing a product or service sales department is a very sensitive department for them. Hence it is very important to keep track of all the records related to sales in the business organization. DBMS is used to maintain records of store customers, products, and sales information in the sales department.

Airlines and Trains

Airlines and Trans are two areas where there is a reservation system, where data is stored which is to be used in the future, so proper data management is very important in these areas. DBMS is used to maintain the records of reservation and schedule information in these areas.

Universities

DBMS is used in universities to maintain records of student information, course registration, college, examination, research work, etc.

Telecommunications

Telecom is also a very prominent to implement DBMS application as there is a huge amount of data traffic. DBMS is used in telecommunications to maintain all the call records of the subscriber, bills for postpaid connections, balance information of prepaid connections, etc.

Finance

The finance sector is the lifeline of any business organization hence maintenance of financial data is on top priority. This can be done very easily by DBMS so the use of DBMS applications is very common in this area.

DBMS is used in the finance sector to maintain information about the purchase of materials, sales invoices, purchase of financial instruments like stocks and bonds, etc.

6.5 Relevance and role of DBMS in decision making

Database management systems offer two fundamental advantages because of these two advantages the relevance of DBMS can never be overlooked. And it also helps in decision-making process of any business management

Redundancy control

The two main pillars of decision-making are the availability of information and its clarity.

Availability of information means that the information is neither too little nor too much. Both the situations are harmful.

Keeping this in mind, DBMS gives top priority to redundancy control because if the same data is being stored repeatedly, then it does not allow it to happen. The redundancy control reduces the repetition of data. As it happens in abundance in our daily life or traditional file system, we sometimes write the same file or data or information in many different places, due to which there is a lot of problem in accessing them in future. The same information is in many places then it becomes complex and when the information becomes complex then it affects our decision-making ability.

When we have very little information in front of us and it is very clear, then we can make the right decision. In the same way, a program can take the right decision only when it neither has too much information nor too little information. The right decision can be taken only on the basis of accurate information. Normalization is used in database management systems, it has different form designs, although it is a complex subject of computer science, with its help, the whole focus is to control the redundancy of the data. So that it can be kept in mind that the data entry person has not stored the same data in many different places and if so, then DBMS reduces it automatically. We know that many times tables are used to store data in an institution, once the table is created, then the data is kept in it, sometimes if another table is needed in the future, then whatever is not understood. When it comes in, a new table is created and it is often seen that many times the same data is in many tables.

Like the joining date of an employee; when someone joins the company for the first time, it is entered into a new table. But as it gets old, a new table is also created for many other tasks and it also has a column of joining dates. If seen, then one entry is done in many different tables, due to this, as the employee gets older, more often the same data (joining date does not change), he gets used again and again, due to which it becomes unnecessary. It wastes time and space. At the same time, with the increase of information, its complexity also increases. So the database management system focuses on the fact that it should remove all the unnecessary data which is in many tables, mainly this responsibility is of the database management database administrator. A database export person handles this. Due to this feature, firstly, very little space is required to store data, less storage is used and secondly, it provides a lot of convenience in processing. Because the data is stored in fewer tables, then it takes less time to access and it is also more convenient, in this way we can say that due to data redundancy control, DBMS remains relevant even today. And its usefulness can never be less in future also.

Data consistency

This is also a unique feature of the database management system because in today's date, while computer science has made a lot of progress, the Internet has developed; we can access the same data from many different places.

Maintaining data consistency is a difficult challenge. A key principle of database management systems is maintaining data consistency. That is, it is the responsibility of the DBMS to keep the data in its consistent state and at the same time, there can never be any disturbance in the data due to this. When we access data from more than one place then there can be many types of problems and if it was not for database management then despite the development of the internet we would not be able to access the data from any different place.

The best example of this is seen in the banking system, today we can do banking transactions from anywhere, either by going to the branch and doing money transactions or withdrawing money from ATMs, this work can be done with the help of internet banking. But one thing is common in all these places; that is the user's database.

This can be understood with an example, suppose Rs.100000 in Ajay's account. Ajay goes to the bank branch and withdraws all money and at the same time, he gives his ATM card to Vijay. Now suppose such a situation comes that Ajay and Vijay together withdraw money at the same time. So there can be a possibility that Rs.100000 Withdrawal can be done from both sides. In that case, you can understand that it is a good sign for Ajay but how big a problem it can create for the bank. The database management system is prepared in advance for this type of situation if there is database management software in the banking system, and then it takes care that the database should never lose its consistency state in such a situation.

This can also be understood with the help of another example, suppose Ajay has ? 100000 in his account and he transfers ? 10000 to Vijay. Vijay's account balance should be increased by ? 10000. The principle of data consistency states that the transaction is either completely completed or not. Because suppose half the transaction happened and ? 10000 was deducted from Ajay's account but ? 10000 didn't come in Vijay's account. Such a situation may come, so the database management system pays great attention to consistency, because of this, there can never be any error in a database because the data is important in decision making, and the database management system guarantees that If a transaction will either be completed or not. There is no place in the database management system for incomplete transactions. For this reason, today it is used in many places from education to industry to banking to the stock market.

Exercises

Objective type question

Choose the correct answer for the followings

Exercises

Objective type question

Choose the correct answer for the followings

1. DBMS is very useful in which of the following sector
(a)Education (b) industry (c) non-profit organization (d) all of these
2. Which of the following is not an advantage of DBMS
(a) Data redundancy control (b) data security (c) Data consistency control (d) data damage control
3. Data redundancy means
(a) Repetition of same data (b) reduce the size of data (c) resize the data (d) all of these
4. In DBMS "partial transaction is not allowed" which of the following DBMS property fulfill the statement?
(a)Data redundancy (b) data consistency (c) Data independence (d) all of these
5. The basic purpose of using DBMS application is
(a) Record maintenance (b) Record keeping (c) Record recovery (d) all of these
6. Why does the relevance of DBMS software persist today
(b) Because of its tools (b) because of its cost (c) because of its demand (d) all of these
7. Which of the following DBMS feature is helpful in decision making?
(a)Data redundancy (b) data consistency (c) Data independence (d) data sharing
8. Which of the following DBMS feature is helpful to reduce the cost of data storage?
(a)Data redundancy (b) data consistency (c) Data independence (d) none of these
9. A table of any DBMS can be accessed by many users. It can be done using
(a)Data redundancy (b) data access (c) data sharing (d) none of these

10. In which of the following is the utility of DBMS the most?

(A) Where the high volume of data is used (b) where data is an important issue (c) where data is related to real persons (d) all of these

Theoretical questions

1. What do you mean by redundancy control? Explain why it is necessary for DBMS?
2. Define data consistency. Describe how it is helpful in internet banking?
3. What are the advantages of the DBMS approach?
4. Describe the relevance of DBMS in business organizations.
5. Explain any two prominent areas of DBMS applications.
6. List and explain the applications of DBMS.
7. Discuss the usage of DBMS in decision-making process.

CHAPTER SEVEN

DATABASE LANGUAGES

In this chapter, we are going to know about various aspects of programming languages in the light of DBMS.

7.1 Programming Languages

To understand the meaning of programming language, we must understand the meaning of program, programming, and language.

What is Programming?

The process of writing a program is called programming.

What is the program?

A program is a set of instructions to solve any given problem and to perform any particular task.

We follow certain instructions to solve a given problem or to perform a task. The set of instructions is called a program.

We also use it in performing various types of daily life activities.

Like when we wake up in the morning, we think about the activities of the day, where to go today? To whom do you want to meet? What to talk about? Start working accordingly. At the same time, if there is any interruption, then we also make some changes in our program.

Along with the activities of daily life, programs are also used in many other areas, such as the basic operations of mathematics (addition, subtraction, multiplication, or division) with the help of the program itself. We do the basic operations of mathematics on the basis of the instructions already learned. A person who does not know about these basic operations of math will not be able to do multiplication and division of two numbers because he does not have the knowledge of the instructions due to which addition, subtraction, multiplication, and division are done.

The main purpose of the program is to write the process of solving a problem in such a way that any person can follow it and solve the problem easily, even if he does not know the solution to that problem in the past.

Suppose a person knows how to multiply two digits numbers but does not know how to multiply three digits numbers, if the same person is explained the method of multiplying three-digit numbers, then the person, who could not multiply three digits numbers before, now can do. Suppose a person does not know how to see a dictionary of English, but when he is explained how to see the dictionary, then he can see the dictionary.

How to multiply a three-digit number or read a dictionary is just a program.

A program is nothing but a method of doing a task. The only difference between a normal program and a computer program is that we humans only understand or explain the normal program, whereas the computer program is written with the help of any programming language. The main purpose of a general program is to make a person understand the method of doing a task whereas the main purpose of a computer program is to get some work done by the computer.

With the help of the program, we can solve any problem or learn new work. If seen, the meaning of learning is to incorporate a new program in itself. Like humans, programs are needed to get work done by computer. Also, computers cannot do any work without a program, so it is inevitable to use a program to get new work done by computer.

What is language?

Language is a medium of communication.

With the help of any language two people, devices can communicate.

If we say it in other words we can say that the language we use to convey our message to someone else is called language. Language can be in any form and it can be written, it can be spoken or it can be a sign or language can be used in different ways in different situations in different ways. But the main purpose of language is to establish communication.

Programming Language:

After understanding the meaning of program, programming, and language, now we understand programming language.

If we want to do something with the help of a computer which the computer is not capable of doing now, it means that we do not have the necessary software to do it. Suppose we want to draw a picture, then first we will find the application program (for example MS-paint) related to making the picture on the computer because without it, we cannot do paint-related work. Now you cannot do drawing or painting in Notepad, right!

Therefore, if we want to work from the computer, then we definitely need some program for that. If there is such a program then it is okay to use it, after installing we can use it. But if there is no software available to do that task, then a new program will have to be written for that because any software is made with the help of the program itself.

We have come to know that to do any new task or to solve any problem, the program is very important, without knowing the program, we cannot solve any problem and neither can do any new task. At the same time, we also know that without language we cannot communicate our words to others.

Based on the above description, we can understand that a program is very much needed to solve any problem. Therefore, if we want to solve a problem through a computer, then surely the computer should also understand the program, on the basis of which it can solve any problem. Or can do a new task. Now the question arises how to explain this program to the computer?

We know that language is needed to explain our point to others, that's why we need a language so that we can transmit our program to the computer.

That is, to get a task done by the computer, the computer has to explain the program, and to explain the program, we need a language that the computer can understand. Since the computer is a machine, it cannot understand our language and we cannot understand the language of the computer, so there is a need for some technology that acts as an intermediary between these two. Mainly the function of programming language is to convert the program written by us into computer language and understand it to the computer. Then the computer can do new tasks based on that and solve new problems. Whatever work we want to do from the computer, we get it done with the help of the program itself.

Whether it is working on MS-Word, painting on paintbrush, any game, table of Excel, or database management software, more programs are needed to do all the work.

Programming language is a computer language that is used by the programmer to explain man-made instructions to the computer. In simple words, the language which is used to give instruction to the computer is called programming language. Programming language is used to develop software.

7.2 Program Development Life Cycle

Program is a base for all kinds of operations performed by the computer or human being.

a computer is identified only by its program because a computer does any work with the help of software, and software is nothing but a collection of programs. With the help of programs written on the computer, the computer performs all types of work. Therefore, it is very important to write the program in the right way because if the program is wrong, you will not be able to achieve the purpose for which the program is written Therefore, the usefulness of the computer and the efficiency of the computer in a way depending on the efficiency of the program. While we have come to know that all the operations of the computer are done with the help of the program itself, from this it can be easily said that the computer itself does not do anything but the program gets that work done. We write programs so that the computer can solve that particular problem.

In this way, it is very clear that the computer does any work because of the program itself. Therefore, the more correct our program, the more useful the computer will be for us, so it is very important for the program to be correct.

The main objective of the Program Development Life Cycle is to teach how to write a program step by step. Because if any work is done systematically then it is more effective and the chances of mistakes are less. Because it is often seen that if we do any work in a systematic way, then that work is done in the right way and we can get the maximum benefit from it.

For example, if someone has to build a house and he starts the work without any planning (planning of the house, management of materials, interior design, consulting with an engineer, arrangement of labor, etc.), then understand how much trouble it will cause. Here the house is just an example, planning before starting any project is called the systematic approach. The bigger or more complex the project, the more will be the need for a systematic approach.

PDLC is a systematic approach to developing computer programs. With its help, writing programs is very convenient. It is essentially used by big software development companies.

There are five stages involved in the program development life cycle. Which are as follows.

Start
Implementation
Testing
Coding
Design
Analysis

Program development life cycle

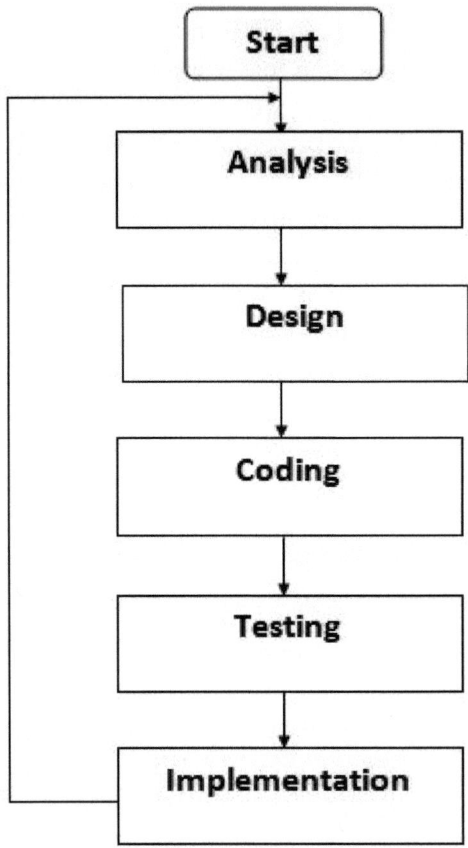

Program development life cycle

Analysis

This is the first stage of the program development life cycle. At this stage, we must have to know the clear and proper definition of the given problem. It is obvious that before going to solve the problem we must have to know about the problem itself. If we don't know about the problem how can we solve this? So before going to write a program to solve any specific problem or to perform any specific task we have to know a very clear definition of that.

Before doing any work, we must know what we have to do? Because if you do not know what to do, then you will not be able to do any work properly and if you don't know exactly what to do and start the work, then there will be more chances of it being wrong. If the program becomes wrong and later it comes in the wrong place, then both time and money are wasted. In order to avoid such wastage, it should be clear at the very beginning of the work what we want, even if the work starts a little late, but the work should be done in the right direction.

So it is very necessary to know about the problem itself before going to take any step towards the solution. Without knowing the problem or solving it with half-incomplete information, nothing will be gained except a waste of time. The success of the whole program was very much dependent on the analysis of the problem itself.

Suppose we want to make a program to print a table of two. To create a program, one must first know what a table is called. It means the complete definition of the table.

Without knowing about every detail of the table we cannot take further steps towards writing the program.

Design

This is the second stage of the program development life cycle. It is also called the solution stage. After completing this stage we must have the solution to the given problem.

After clearing the definition of the problem, it is the turn that how to solve the problem? A programmer (a person who writes a program) finds a solution to a problem with the help of logic and his own experience and similar programs in the past. Logic has the most important role in solving any problem. The better the logic of the program, the more effective its program will be.

Basically to get the solution to the given problem is based on the ability of the programmer. There is no specific tool for getting the solution. Because of only the design stage, the involvement of human beings still exists in the field of computer science.

Logic representation tool

The logic of problem-solving arises mainly in the mind of the programmer because of his reasoning ability and skill.

We should not forget that our aim here is not to solve the problem but to solve the problem with the computer. So only the logic of problem-solving is not enough. After the solution to the problem is found, there is also a need for representation.

The main purpose of the Logic Representation Tool is to represent the logic of the programmer in the form so that any third person (even a computer) can solve the problem with the help of the logic used by the programmer.

Algorithms

It is a logical representation tool.

An algorithm is a set of rules to be followed in a problem-solving operation.

The algorithm is a step-by-step demonstration of data processing or problem-solving.

Therefore an algorithm is a set of rules or instructions that define step by step how a task is to be performed in order to achieve the expected result.

This can be understood with the example of making a new recipe. When we make a new recipe, we go through the instructions and steps and execute them one by one in the given sequence. Algorithms designed are language-independent i.e. it is just simple instructions that can be implemented in any language

With the help of an algorithm, the programmer can explain his logic by writing it in a common language. With the help of this, any person who cannot solve the problem can solve the problem with the help of an algorithm. The aim is to explain the method to solve the problem. Directly or indirectly we use algorithms to solve any problem or to accomplish any task. The only difference is that we may have memorized the algorithm. We don't need to read it from anywhere. But many times it happens that when a new type of problem comes, then we look for its solution. Mostly the solution of a problem or how to do a task is explained only with the help of an algorithm.

This is the most used tool to represent logic because we do not need any special training or any extra effort to use it.

We simply write down the solution step by step.

While writing an algorithm, special care should be taken that it is being written for another person. So it should be very clear that there should not be any doubts.

Flow chart

A flowchart is a graphical tool of problem-solving steps.

Different symbols are used for different types of instructions. And inside it, the instructions are written in brief. The direction of execution of the instruction is indicated by the symbol of the arrow. This makes the program very easy to explain and it is also easy to correct mistakes.

Many times the logic of the program is so complex that it is not convenient to represent it with the help of a common language.

Flow chart symbols

The flow chart is a pictorial presentation tool of program logic.

Some standard symbols used in flow chart

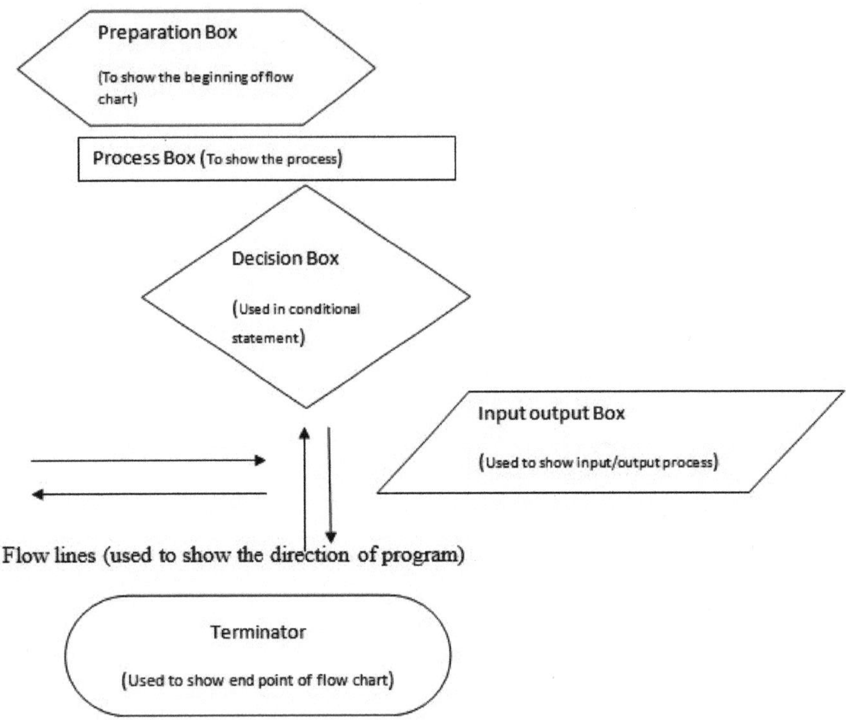

Enter Caption

The standard symbol is used to create a flowchart. Any person in the world who makes a flow chart or reads it can easily understand the meaning of those symbols. Hence flow charts made internationally are easier to create and understand.

With the help of a flowchart, it is easy to understand and explain the logic of the program. In fact, the purpose of writing a program is to explain your program to someone else. So whoever has prepared the solution of the program needs to know the flowchart. It is not that the logic of the program cannot be explained without a flowchart, but with the help of a flow chart, even the most difficult logic can be explained in a very easy and effective way. It is rightly said that

A picture is worth a thousand words.

Sometimes a small diagram says many things instead of many words. That's why flow charts are considered a very effective tool for logic presentation.

Coding

We can mainly divide the program development life cycle into two parts. Analysis and design come in the first part. In this part, we mainly analyze the problem and prepare the blueprint of the solution.

The main objective of the first step is to prepare a framework to solve the problem. The second part of PDLC works on the basis of this framework.

The second phase of PDLC is computer-based. The computer world starts from this phase.

If seen, any person who has the ability to solve the problem is useful for the first phase. But to work in the second phase, knowledge of computer language or programming language is necessary. As already discussed, the main purpose of language is to communicate its point of view to others. Here we mean to explain to the computer the blueprint or framework of the program created by the First Phase or the algorithm of the solution. And to explain to the computer, we need some medium that can explain these things to him in his language.

In this stage, the algorithm or the content of the flow chart is converted into a programming language and typed into the computer, which is called coding. Every programming language has its own coding style. Now as the name suggests (Language) and like every language, every programming language also has its own grammar, its own syntax, and its own keyboard. There are different types of programming languages for different situations for different types of different purposes. But the basic objective of all is the same, how to convert algorithms into computer language? Programming languages use compilers or interpreters to perform this task. With its help, the code written by the programmer is converted into machine language. Now the machine performs the process on the basis of the same code. In this way whatever algorithm was written at the design stage is converted into computer language. And we know that algorithms are written for a third person so that anyone can read the algorithm and solve the problem. Now that it is possible to convert algorithms into computer language, so the computer is also able to solve the problem for which the algorithm is written in ordinary language. There are many types of programming languages used in computer science Such as c, c++, java, HTML, python etc. After selecting the appropriate language, the algorithms in that language are changed and coding is done in the program.

The process of converting algorithms to a particular programming language is called coding. Each programming language has a different coding method.

For this, it is necessary for the person who is doing the coding work to have a good knowledge of that programming language.

The main purpose of coding is to convert the program into machine language. For this, a special type of program is used, which is called compiler/interpreter. With their help, the programs written by us in a high-level language are converted into low-level or machine-level language understandable by the computer. And on the basis of that, the computer solves the given problem, like a person after following the algorithm. An algorithm can do what it is written for, in the same way, a computer can do the same thing after coding very fast and without any mistakes. Because humans can make mistakes in following the steps of the algorithm, but the computer cannot.

Basically, the biggest advantage of a computer system is that the instructions are followed very fast and without any mistakes.

Testing

Testing is a process to check whether a program behaves as desired or not, through actual execution. The program is executed and supplied with test data, and the way a program reacts to this test data is analyzed and the desired improvements are made to the program.

In this step, we check whether the algorithm or coding that is written and for which it is written serves the purpose. Simply put, checking whether our algorithmic flowchart or coding is correct or not is called testing because it is not sensible to implement the program directly without testing it. Therefore, first of all, programs, algorithms, logic, or coding are all tested first. There are various tools to test. It is a subject of computer science. Different types of tools like black-box testing, white box testing, etc. test the program with the help of a variety of techniques. If no defects are found in it then we proceed to the next step. But if any fault is found then it is removed, this process is called debugging.

? the process of removing bugs is called debugging.

Many times computer programmers ignore this step but we must not forget that doing systematic work gets the job done properly and the basic purpose of the program development life cycle is to write the program systematically. And a systematic approach says that the program should be checked before direct implementation and this is actually a very wise move. For example, you've developed an algorithm that solves a problem, so before you tell that algorithm to the world, you'll want to test it out in different ways because if you once told someone and He will find fault in that. If he does so, you will be greatly insulted. So it is wise to test your algorithm first. Scientific people also make great use of testing. The success or failure of any experiment is decided on this level. Because sometimes it seems that our program or experiment was successful, but with the help of different types of equipment adopted in the test, we can find out the shortcomings which are usually not understood. For example, if someone makes a water ship and drops it directly into the water, then there is a problem in it, then the ship will sink and so much time, money, and labor will be wasted. Therefore the ship should be tested without being lowered into the water with the help of various tools, only after that it should be lowered into the water. This is an example, with the help of which we can understand the importance of testing.

Implementation

In this stage, the purpose for which we write the program, that purpose is fulfilled. For example, if a person places an order for a company to get the software made of the bank, then the company uses all the stages of the program development life cycle. After the success of the testing stage, we can finally install that program or software by going to that bank so that now the bankers can use the software made by that company/person. Because their purpose was to make software for the bank and that purpose is not possible until the software is installed by going to the bank. Therefore, without the implementation stage, our entire program is meaningless. Therefore, this is the most final and most important stage of program development. Because the user does not have any meaning with the steps of writing our program or testing it or what problems he has seen in it, he only means with his program. The person who makes the final use of the program is called the end-user. The only thing that means to the end-user is whether the work we wanted to get done from the computer is now being done by the computer or not? The main purpose of making a computer program is to get that work done by the computer. Finally, it is seen whether that particular task is now being done by the computer or not, and if it is happening then it is installed in the computer. In the computer world, the implementation process is also called installation. This can be considered to be a shipwreck. Then what is the use of building a ship until the ship is not lowered into the water? Some people also associate the implementation stage with the maintenance state.

After some time after implementation, our system starts running. Our software starts running after some time requires maintenance. Because when the program is written, the situation at that time is different, after some time the time changes further. Changes come in many things. As there are changes in the bank interest rate, the fare in a train, bus, rail keeps on increasing, the tax rate keeps on changing. Therefore, the coding of the program also has to be changed. Or after some time some such problem comes which cannot be detected in testing, it is caught only when our software is installed. It is necessary to fix it after some time interval. This process is called maintenance. For this, the process is started again from the analysis state because whatever new problem has come up or whatever changes have to be made, it has to be understood again, then it has to be designed, then it has to be coding then it has to be tested and implement it in the last. Still some time passes, then the analysis is done, design is done, coding is done and after testing, it is implemented again. So this process goes on continuously as long as the software is used. That is why the term cycle is used along with program development because it is a continuous process that goes on again and again.

Example:

To better understand the whole process of PDLC we can take the help of a problem i.e.

Problem: how to print the table of a given number.

Stage 1: ANALYSIS:

We know that at this stage we must have a clear definition of the given problem. We must have know what to do before how to do it?

After completing the analysis of the given problem we have the result ....

"Table writing is the process of multiplying the given number with one and showing the product. Again, multiply the given number by two and show the product. Multiply the given number with three and show the product. Repeat this process again and again until the multiplier reaches 10."

Stage 2: Design

Finding the solution to the problem i.e. how to print the table of a given number?

Solution:

Algorithm
START
Step 1: Read the value of given number.
Step 2: Initialize i with 1.
Step 3: While i is less than 11, perform the step 4 otherwise go-to stop.
Step 4: Multiply the given number with i and show the product.
Increment i with one.
Go-to step 3
STOP
Flow chart
Shows how to print the table of a given number

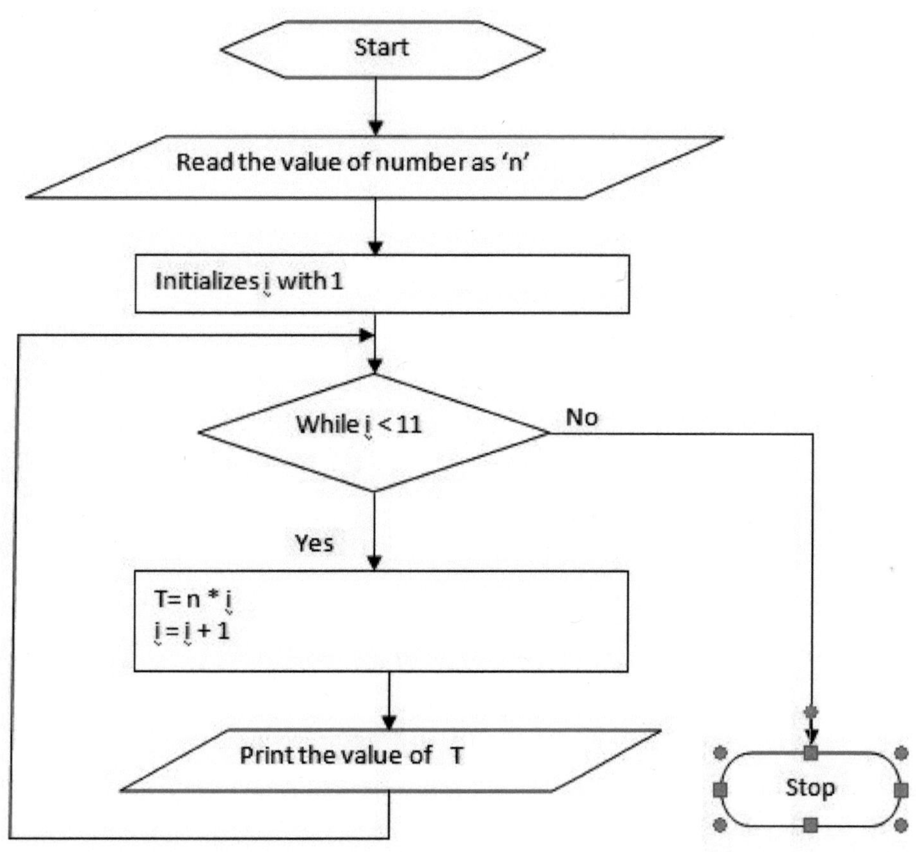

Shows how to print the table of a given number

Stage 3: Coding

A computer program in c language to print the table of a given number.

```
#include < stdio.h >
int main()
{
int n, i = 1;
printf("Enter a number\n");
```

```
scanf("%d", &n);
printf("\nMultiplication table for %d is:\n\n", n);
while( i < 11 )
{
printf("%d x %d = %d\n", n, i, (n*i));
i = i + 1;
}
return 0;
}
```

Computer screen

Stage 4: Testing

Let the value of n is 5

5
10
15
20
25
30
35
40
45
50

i = 1
T= n * i i = i + 1
i < 11 case true T= 5 * 1 i = 1 + 1
= 5 =2
i < 11 case true T= 5 * 2 i = 2 + 1
= 10 =3
i < 11 case true T= 5 * 3 i = 3 + 1
= 15 =4
i < 11 case true T= 5 * 4 i = 4 + 1
= 20 =5
i < 11 case true T= 5 * 5 i = 5 + 1
= 25 =6
i < 11 case true T= 5 * 6 i = 6 + 1
= 30 =7
i < 11 case true T= 5 * 7 i = 7 + 1
= 35 =8
i < 11 case true T= 5 * 8 i = 8 + 1
= 40 =9
i < 11 case true T= 5 * 9 i = 9 + 1
= 45 =10
i < 11 case true T= 5 * 10 i = 10 + 1
= 50 = 11
i < 11 case false
Program terminated

Stage 5: Implementation

To implement this program install the program into the computer. And use it.

7.3 Types of Programming Languages

The basic purpose of any programming language is to convert high-level language (humans can understand) into the machine-level language (computer can understand).

But one thing should also be remembered that every programming language has a specialized field.

Every programming language has a purpose. Keeping in mind the same purpose, any programming language is made. Today the field of computer is very wide. Today computer is used in the banking sector, in gaming, in telecommunication, in data processing, in railways, in airline reservation systems, in system designing, in face recognition, in voice recognition, in ATM machines, in aeronautics, in the entertainment industry, etc. If a computer is used to do any work, it means that that work will be done by some programs. Because we know that the computer does any work through the program itself. Therefore, different types of programs are also required to perform different types of tasks. Not all types of programs can be written by the same programming language. To write a particular kind of program, a particular kind of programming language is required. That's why there are many types of programming languages. Following are some of the main programming language types

Markup Language: HTML, XML, WML etc. are examples of some markup languages. A markup language is used to design the web page of the website. Whenever you go to a website, a page is present in front of you, that page is called a webpage. And the programming language used to create that page is called markup language.

Scripting Languages: Some scripting languages like JavaScript, VBScript, etc are examples of this. This is also related to the web page of the Internet. Where markup language is used to display the content on the web page, the same scripting language is used to perform some internal processing some logical activities in the web page.

We know that the Internet client is based on the server model. In this model, the client machine requests for a webpage or for any content from the server machine. This request reaches the server machine in electronic form using the network infrastructure. Now the server on the basis of this electronic request sends the appropriate content back to the client machine again using the same network infrastructure. In this way, the sequence of requests and replies goes on between the client and the server. It is to be noted here that a lot of network infrastructure is used in the process of this request and reply. Network infrastructure Capacity is limited, so it is necessary that the minimum use of network infrastructure is done so that the maximum number of people can use the Internet.

Such tasks related to some web pages that can be processed mainly on the local client's machine, which does not require a server, can be done with the help of scripting language. Suppose a student's mark sheet is to be viewed through the Internet, then the number of different subjects of that student's mark sheet will be stored in the server. Those numbers cannot be accessed without the help of the server but we do not need to reach the server to know the sum of all those subjects. This does not put unnecessary pressure on the server. There are many such tasks on the Internet that can be done on the local machine, they are called local processing. There is minimum pressure on the server on the Internet, there should be minimum load, and the emphasis is on maximum local processing to reduce the network traffic that does not unnecessarily request requests on the server. Programs related to local processing are created with the help of scripting languages.

Server-Side Programming: The Internet is based on the client-server model. We want to access it by typing the URL of a website from our computer's browser. This is a kind of request to the server. This request reaches the server. Now the server designs a web page based on the request received by the client and sends it to the client. The web pages to be developed based on the request of the client are called dynamic web pages. And with the help of server-side programming language dynamic pages are created. Examples of server-side programming languages are JSP, PHP, and ASP, etc.

Systems Programming: Some programming languages like c, c++ are used for system programming. Systems programming means creating programs that a computer system uses for itself. That does not interact with the user. This means that the user does not use this type of program directly. The user never knows when this type of program is used. Without these programs, our computer system cannot even function. As we know that there are two types of software, system software, and application software. Although application programs can also be created with the help of c, c++, they are specially used for systems programming, they are also called general-purpose programming languages. Various programs can be created with their help.

Database Programming: Among the many types of computer functions, database management is one of the main functions. The computer has to perform many types of operations related to the database. There are many types of software available for this. Such as Oracle MS Access etc., with the help of these, many database tasks can be done. But with this software, we can do only that which is already present in it. If we want to do something new to do a particular type of work or want to do something that is not present in the readymade software, then we or any business organization can make new database management software according to its requirement. . Because any type of software can be created with the help of programming language.

Therefore, many times many business organizations make separate database-related software for themselves. Database management software can be made with the help of database programming language FoxPro dBase PL/SQL etc. are examples of database programming languages. With the help of these, we can create or make different types of database software as per our requirements.

A programming language that is used to design and develop a database-based application is called a database programming language such as FoxPro,dBase, PL/SQL, etc.

A very popular domain-specific database language (Structured Query Language SQL) is also used to manage and manipulate relational databases. Programmers use SQL statements to perform various tasks in database applications like SQL Server, MySQL, Oracle, MS-Access, and many other popular databases.

7.4 Database Languages

Database language is an organized collection of statements, which are used to define and manipulate a database.

Database language is used to perform various data-related tasks such as creating and storing data in a computer system. DBMS itself is one of the biggest futures of database language which is a software application that is used to manage data with the help of database language.

For whatever work the database administrator wants to do related to the database, he needs the language of the database because any DBMS software understands the language of the database itself.

So the database administrator communicates with the DBMS using the database language. In general, the instructions given to the DBMS are called queries in the database language.

If seen, database language is a special tool provided by DBMS, with the help of which a database administrator can create a new database as per his requirement and fetch desired data from the stored database. The database language also facilitates modification and transformation of query results by average, count, sum, etc. The database language enables the user's interaction with other applications.

Basically, any database language consists of the following two languages. In other words, we can say that database language can be classified mainly into two parts.

DDL (Data Definition Language)

DML (Data Manipulation Language)

DDL

The first function of any database is its creation. The use of DDL is related to the creation of the database. Functions related to the database, which are related to the earliest stage of the database, come under DDL. DDL is used to define the database as well as DDL is also used to define the Conceptual Schema.

DDL is a very important part of the database language because it forms the basic structure of the database. And all the further process depends on it. For example, when we create a table for any work, the first task is to specify the name of the table, the heading of the column of the table, the number of columns, etc. Once the table is created, then only entry has to be done in it. Once records are inserted in the table then it is not possible to change the design of the table. That is why the place of DDL is paramount in DBMS language.

The commands used to define the database are called DDL commands, under DDL we can create tables, change the name of the table or delete the table. We can also specify the data type of a field. Suppose that there is a field 'mobile number' in 'student basic information table' so we can restrict the user to only enter numbers values in that field.

The following are the some main commands of Data Definition Language: -

> Create

> Alter
> Drop
> Create Command
This command is used to create a table for a database.
Syntax:-
Create Table <tablename>
(field name1 datatype , field name2 datatype
);
Example:-
Create Table student
(name varchar(20) , address varchar(20)
);

After executing create command DBMS create a table with the name student and has two fields (column) i.e. name, address varchar(20) is a data type that specifies whether the entry of the name should be a character, number, or special character. 20 means the length of the field. Meaning the value of that field (name, address in given example) cannot be more than 20 characters long.

char(size), varchar (size),date,time,year,real,double,AutoNumber etc. are some other common data types that are frequently used.

> Alter
With the help of alter command we can do the followings

- Add new field(column) in the existing table
- Change the data type of a field
- Existing column can be deleted
- Rename the fields
- Drop a column

To add new field in existing table
Syntax:-
ALTER Table <tablename>
ADD <column name>datatype
Example:-
ALTER Table student
ADD class varchar(20) ;
Multiple columns can also be added at once.
ALTER Table tablename
ADD <column_name1> datatype , <column_name2> datatype, <column_name3> datatype, ... <column_name n> datatype ;
Example
ALTER Table student
ADD Father_Name varchar(20), roll_number varchar(10),city varchar(10) ;

After executing the alter command 3 new fields will be added in the existing table student. and now the structure of student table is look like..

Student

Name | Address | Class | Father_name | Roll_number | City

To Drop A field
Syntax:-

ALTER TABLE tablename
DROP COLUMN <fieldname>
Example:-
ALTER TABLE student
DROP COLUMN class;
After executing this, the class field will be removed from the table. And the structure of the table looks like...
Student

Name | Address | Father_name | Roll_number | City
To Change Column Data Type
Syntax:-
ALTER TABLE <tablename>
MODIFY columname newdatatype
Example:-
ALTER TABLE student
MODIFY roll_number int;
After executing this command the data type of roll_number column will be changed from varchar to int.
To Rename Column Name
Syntax:-
ALTER TABLE <tablename>
CHANGE COLUMN old_name TO new_name;
Example:-
ALTER TABLE student
CHANGE COLUMN name TO student_name;
after executing this command the name of the field name 'name' is changed to 'student_name' and the structure of the table looks like...
Student

Student_name | Address | Father_name | Roll_number | City
To Rename the Table Name
Syntax:-
ALTER TABLE <old_table_name>
RENAME TO <new_table_name>
Example:-
ALTER TABLE student
RENAME TO student_data;
after executing this command table structure is lokk like this ..
Student_data

Student_name | Address | Father_name | Roll_number | City
> DROP
DROP command is used to delete a table
Syntax:–
DROP TABLE tablename;
Example:-
DROP TABLE student_data;
After executing this command the complete 'student_data' table will be removed from the disk.
DML (Data Manipulation Language)

Where the work of DDL was to design the structure of the database, the work of DML is to insert data into it after the structure is ready.

The main function of DML is to insert, edit/update, or delete records in the database.

This is also a very important part of the database language because the content of our database is inserted in the database only through DML. If we have to make any changes in that content, then work can be done with the help of DML only.

DDL is in a way like a blank notebook whereas DML is the words written in that blank notebook.

Where on one hand the work of DDL is to prepare the structure of a blank notebook, on the other hand, the task of DML is to write the content in a prepared blank notebook.

Therefore, both have an important place in the database language.

But from the point of view of the user, DML contributes more because the user is only concerned with his data.

For example, if your account is in a bank, then how the bank maintains your account does not matter to you, what matters to you is the account of your money.

There should be no mistake in that.

That is why Data Manipulation Language plays a very sensitive role in DBMS because if there is something wrong with the user's content, then it is a very dangerous sign for the DBMS. This is because it is the most primary fundamental responsibility of any DBMS to store, maintain, access, and secure the user's content (records). So it should always be correct.

DML is also used to view some selected records (to access only desired information instead of viewing the full) from the stored database. This process is known as query processing in the language of DBMS.

Query: Retrieving only the records you want from the entire database. Like information related to the whole world has been given in a table but we want to get information about India only.

Query processing is an integral part of a database management system.

Generally, any business organization uses a database management system because of query processing because earlier it was the most difficult task to find desired records from very large databases. And this work is done because of DML in DBMS.

That is why DML can also be called a synonym for Database Language.

Because from the point of view of the user, whatever work is done related to the database, such as storing the data and getting the desired records from them from time to time, is done through DML only.

Due to DML, we or any user can easily search whatever data we want to search from a huge amount of databases using some simple syntax.

Suppose there are 10,000 employees working in a company. Someday suddenly the manager needs information about such employee or employees whose salary is more than 1,00,000, who also take more than 10 consecutive days of leave, and whose age is more than 55 years, in this situation in normal way this It would have been quite difficult to find these kinds of complex records. With the help of DML, DBMS gives the user the facility to handle complex to most complex queries that too at very fast speed and without any mistake.

A good database user is considered to be one who can use the DML language as efficiently as possible. That is, as efficiently as one can write the query because if the database administrator does not know how to use DML then he cannot use the database management system efficiently.

In other words, we can say that efficient use of Database Management systems can be done by those people who can use DML efficiently. And DML can be used efficiently by only those who can write queries well. The one who writes good queries is called a good database administrator.

With the help of DML the following main task can be performed.

> inserting records into the table

> Finding selected records from a table.

> updating the records of the table

> deleting the records from the table

DML Commands

The following are some very common and useful DML commands.

> Select

> Insert

> Update

> Delete

> **Select Command**

The select command is used to select the row in the table of the database.

Syntax:-

SELECT column1 , colum2........columnN FROM tablename

Example:-

SELECT roll_number , name FROM student;

After executing this command, the only roll_number and name row of the student table will be displayed in the output.

à If we want to select all rows then we can use * sign in place of any column name.

Syntax

SELECT * FROM <table name>;

Example

SELECT * FROM student;

---> After executing this command all records of the student table will be displayed on the screen.

---> with the use of 'where' keyword we can filter the result on the basis of some given criteria such as Find the name of those students whose age is greater than 20, so to do this we can query like..

Example

Select name from student

Where age > 20;

After executing this, the name of those students will be displayed whose age is greater than 20.

Example

Select * from student

Where age>20;

After executing this, all fields (all columns of table) of those students will be displayed whose age is greater than 20.

> **Insert Command**

With the help of the insert command, we can insert values in the table of the database.

Syntax:-

For all columns

INSERT INTO <tablename >VALUES (value1, value2, value3.................value n);

→ n is the maximum value of the table column. It must be the same as column number.suppose there are 5 columns in any table and in that case the value of n must be 5. and order is also the same as the actual table.

For specified column

INSERT INTO <tablename> (column1, column 2,....column n)

VALUES (value1, value2, value3.................value n);

→ Here the value of n is dependent on the user's requirement but it should be the same in both parameters of tablename() and values ().

Example:-

For all columns

INSERT INTO student data VALUES ('AJAY KUMAR','2C/86 sector 9 van vihar','NEELKANTH KUMAR',21108001,'varanasi);

For specified column

INSERT INTO student_data(student_name,Roll_number)

VALUES ('vikas yadav', 21108002);

After executing this the table looks like...

Student_data

Student_name | Address | Father_name | Roll_number | City

AJAY KUMAR | 2C/86 sector 9 van vihar | NEELKANTH KUMAR | 21108001 | varanasi

vikas yadav | | | 21108002 |

> Update Command

Using the update command, we can change any new value from the existing value in the table of the database.

Syntax:-

UPDATE tablename

SET columnname = value, columname2= value

Where <condition>;

Example:-

UPDATE student

SET name= 'rohit dixit', father_name='vikas dixit'

Where roll_number = 21108001;

After executing this name of roll number 21108001 will be changed/update form ajay kumar to rohit dixit as well as father name from neelkanth kumar to vikas dixit.

> if you do not use the where statement in the update command all records will be updated.

> Delete Command

The delete command is used to delete the records/touples of the tables of the database. And we can also delete multiple records with delete command

Syntax:-

DELETE FROM tablename;

Example:-

DELETE FROM student;

After executing this all records of the student table will be removed from disk.

7.5 dBase package

dBase is a data base management software package.

dBase is a powerful database system for storing, organizing, analyzing and accessing information on a computer.

dBASE is an older but fairly popular database software application that can be used on your personal computer to help organize and maintain your database files. It's actually a set of many tools by which you can create, access, organize, select, delete and manipulate data in a very simple and effective way.

It provides an integrated environment for the database users to perform various database-related tasks such as providing a user-friendly interface to store access and manipulating data, providing programming facilities to its user so that they can do such tasks which are not inbuilt in the package, providing facility to update software itself from time to time so that its user can get the benefit of new research happening in the field of DBMS. This feature of any standard software package is that where on the one hand it provides all the facilities available to its user along with the package, at the same time it should also provide the facility to do the work which is not in the software. And such tasks can be done only with the help of programming language. The programming section of the dBase software package is so powerful that dBase is often considered a programming language.

dBase is a specialized software package used to create and edit /update /manipulate relational databases. The term may also refer to the dBase database programming language that first appeared in the dBase product, but which is also available today in many other database forms.

As a DBMS software package, dBase was the very first commercially successful database system for personal computers and is one of the most widely used other database software packages.

Today many versions of dBase have come into the market like dBase II, III, III Plus and dBase IV, dBase Plus 8, etc.

In early versions of dBase, to create a database or search for data, edit, update, delete, or perform any number of other tasks, you had to type commands on the command line, as you do in MS-DOS. It was also referred to as CUI (Character User Interface). Nowadays, you can do a lot of things using a menu-driven interface (sometimes referred to as a graphical user interface). Working with a GUI is much easier. Using the dBase programming language, it is very easy to use a program written by someone else. With the help of this, not only the program created by yourself but also others can be installed in your system, which increases the portability of the program. And any program becomes even more useful for us. People who know dBase can write complete programs to carry out customized tasks such as managing your company's inventory, invoicing systems, and customer inventory. Once the program is working properly, one can run it without knowing anything about dBase commands. After the program is installed, any normal person can use dBase easily, for this he does not need much technical knowledge. Although the dBase programming language originated with the dBase software product, it has taken on a life of its own because of the popularity of the language. Many other software makers have also made similar software packages but it has its own special place.

Since the name dBase is associated with a package as a whole, the section of the dBase programming language is often referred to as xBase. dBase is an example of the most powerful relational database management software available today; This includes every feature you need as a database user. dBase allows you to create the structure of your database file immediately and easily. You can create custom data entry forms in no time by using the screen for content generated in dBase. When your data is in the file, you can start converting data into useful information by sorting data or asking questions from the feature known as query-by-example. Apart from asking questions and getting answers, you can also get a fully customized report. dBase has a report writer that allows you to create any programming report you can think of. You can also prepare mailing labels and mail merge documents.

Finally, for those of you who want to build a menu-driven system but are intimidated to program, your fears have been dispelled. dBase has a powerful, yet easy-to-use App generator that allows you to develop quickly with your existing database files, screens, and reports A menu system that will make data entry easy for novice computer operators, even if they haven't used dBase before.

dBase is a relational database-based system which means it can add multiple files together so that they can work as a single file even when they are separated. dBase can relate to your customer file, your invoice file, and your inventory file to provide you with the ability to work with all the data, such as in one file. Changing any type of record can automatically identify and affect the files related to dBase. The simplest system also requires relational database management as per today's demand for constantly changing information. dBase gives you all the facilities of a real database.

The whole package of dBASE can be mainly divided into the following three parts.

Programming:

You can create your own customized, menu-driven (GUI) application by storing the dBASE command in a special program. Automating database systems and using dBASE commands requires the end-user to be proficient in the dBASE command language and have an understanding of basic programming concepts.

The programming part of dBase cannot be used by normal users. It can be used by only those users who have experience in computer programming. Or he has previously worked on any other programming language. But it is not that it is very difficult, any experienced programmer can learn it quickly and easily.

Therefore, dBASE programming is often used only by more advanced users of the application. However, some simple programs can be made even by novice users!

Menu Based Interface: This is the menu-driven interface of dBASE that provides centralized access to all the features and commands of dBASE. It is also called the control center. Control Center is often used by new users to the product because it is very easy to use. Control Center, when used to its full potential, gives you all the power you'll ever need to design, update and maintain your database files. It also provides database security.

Command Line Interface: The dBASE command line provides direct control of command input to the end-user. The command-line interface is also called the character user interface (CUI). Because commands are just a collection of some characters whose definition is already present in the software. The dBASE command language has hundreds of functions and commands that are used to accomplish both simple and complex tasks.

You should have a basic knowledge of the available commands and their syntax, before using the command-line interface of the dBase package.

Exercises

Objective type question

Choose the correct answer for the followings

1. A program is a ___________________.
(a) Collection of data (b) set of instructions (c) collection of information (d) none of these
2. The basic purpose of any language is
(a) communication (b) writing program (c) giving instruction (d) all of these
3. Which of the following is a programming language
(a) C (b) ms-access (c) oracle (d) sql
4. C++, java and html are example of.
(a) DBMS (b) word-processor (c) networking devices (d) programming language
5. Programming languages are used to convert ________ to machine level language.
(a) Binary language (b) Low Level Language (c) High Level Language (d) none of these
6. ___________ is the first stage of program development life cycle.
(a) Design (b) Analysis (c) Testing (d) Coding
7. Algorithm and flow chart are used to
(a) Represent program logic (b) writing program (c) testing the program (d) none of these
8. Black box and white box technique is popular for.
(a) Program testing (b) analyzing problem (c) program control (d) coding
9. Debugging is a process of removing _____ from the program.
(a) comma (b) semi colon (c) repeated lines (d) errors
10. In PDLC the process of coding comes just after
(a) testing (b) design (c) analysis (d) implementation
11. Which of the following programming language is used for developing web pages
(a) C (b) C++ (c) PHP (d) dBase
12. Which of the following is an example of database language
(a) dBase (b) C (c) C++ (d) java
13. DDL and DML are two ___________________
(a) Scripting language (b) System language (c) markup language (d) Database language
14. Which of the following is an example of DDL?
(a) INSERT (b) SELECT (c) CREATE (d) DELETE
15. Which of the following is an example of DML?
(a) INSERT (b) CREATE (c) ALTER (d) DROP

Theoretical questions

1. What do you mean by programming languages? Explain with example.
2. How many stages are there in PDLC? Describe each of them in detail.
3. Draw a flow chart to find the greatest number among the three numbers.
4. Write an algorithm to find the factorial of a given number.
5. Explain different types of programming languages with names.
6. Distinguish between DML and DDL.
7. List and explain the various commands of DML.
8. Write a note on the dBase package.

CHAPTER EIGHT

DATA PROCESSING

In this chapter, we are going to know the basics of data processing.

8.1 Meaning of Data Processing

Data processing is a process of manipulating input data in such a way that the data should be transformed into a more precious, useful and valuable form. Data processing can include any use of a computer processor or application program to perform defined operations on data to produce meaningful and worthy information.

Just like any other system data processing is also a kind of system as we know the system is an orderly grouping of interdependent components linked together according to a plan to achieve a specific goal. In data processing, there are different components like the system, the most important thing about the system is that every system has the main purpose, to achieve that purpose; it has different components which are connected to each other. They are dependent on each other and together they help in achieving that specific goal. In a very simple language, we can say that there are three parts of the system; Input, Process, and Output. Any system in the whole world is made up of these three things. Like our body, trees, plants, animals, trains, buses, engines, cars, bicycles, motorcycles, different types of machines, and a lot more, all are systems. But if seen, they all have different functions but there is one similarity that all are systems. The most fundamental concept is that the system takes input, processes it, and generates output. One thing that makes everyone different that is their objective. Like washing machine is a system and car is also a system but the purpose of a washing machine is to wash clothes and the purpose of a car is to run. It is both systems, Washing machine also needs electricity for input clothes water Detergent, etc. After this, it does the processing and presents the last washed clothes. Similarly, the car needs petrol and after processing this, the result is that it provides movement to the car. Overall, the input process output is there in all systems, but the purpose of processing is different for everyone. On the basis of this purpose, all different types of systems are called systems with a different name; the computer itself is the biggest example of a data processing system.

Every system has a purpose, so to understand any system; we must first understand its purpose that's why it was created. As already mentioned data processing is also a system, its purpose is to collect data and after processing, convert the output into different formats according to the requirement of different applications.

If someone tells you what a computer does? So you can say that computer does data processing and what does it do in data processing? So it depends on the different applications. MS Paint also does the data processing, MS Word also does the processing, Media player also does the processing, If there is any video game software it also does the processing, all these different applications perform processing in different ways and to achieve a different goal.

So we can say that data processing is a process of transforming data into a predefined desired format.

It can be done manually or electronically. In earlier times, the work of data processing was done manually but due to the advent of the computer, now this work is done with the help of a computer. Obviously because of data processing software in computer the work of data processing has become very fast as well as its accuracy also increases. We know that computer hardware alone cannot do anything, but it works only in collaboration with software. We know that a database management system is a useful software for data processing, its main purpose is to do the processing of data but it is not so. That only database management system software can process data, here data processing refers to each such application that processes data and presents the output in different formats in different forms.

The computer does the work of data processing only with the help of software. Therefore different types of software do the work of different types of data processing. We cannot say that data processing is done with any specific software. For example Word processor software is also an example of a data processor because it also does the processing of words; it presents the simple text written by us in different ways in different designs so it is a data processor. There is some software that produces our written word through sound, there; our data is presented in the form of voice. There is much software that presents our data with the help of charts. In this way, there are many different types of software, which produce output after processing the data in different ways, present it in a different format in the desired way; mainly we can say that the purpose of data processing is to make the data more valuable. We have to make it so that it becomes more useful for us.

8.2 Basics of Data Processing Operations

One thing that should always be remembered about the computer is that it is a system and one thing that should always be remembered about the system is that it consists of three basic parts, input process, and output. This means it should also have three components; it will receive the input, do the processing and generate the output. As it is already discussed Data processing is also a system. Basically, it also has three main components; Data collection, performing different types of processes on an individual application basis, and result in submission as per application format.

Data processing tasks can be divided into three parts:

I. Collection of data (input)

II. Process the data

III. Converting to desired format as per application requirement (output)

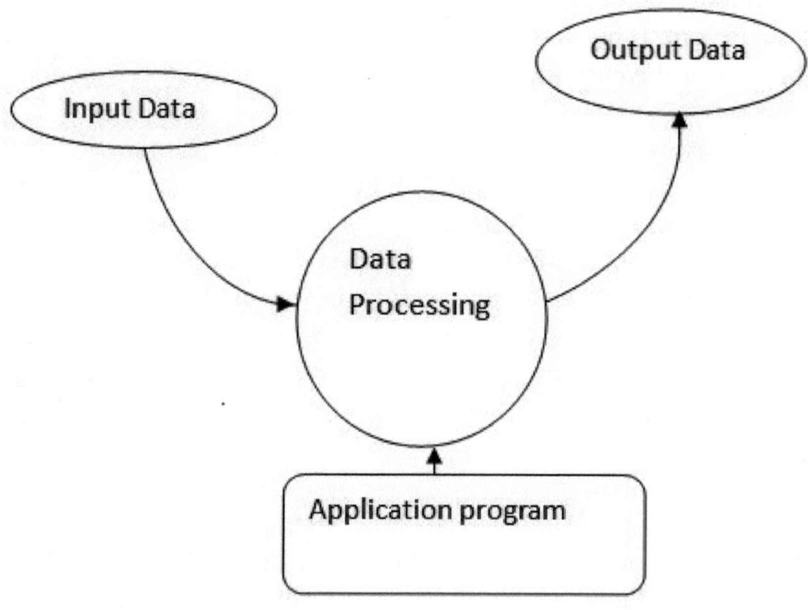

Data Processing

Data Processing
Input Data
Output Data
Application program

I. Collection of data: The first part of data processing is collecting data collection. All data processing work is dependent on data collection because if there is no data how will the processing take place and how to find the result? So the first task is to input the data. Nowadays many websites provide many facilities for free just to collect data like free mail service, free chat, free news, etc. All these websites have only one purpose and that is to take your data. Many offline or online surveys are done to collect data only. The data that we easily provide for free is very valuable for those websites. Their entire business is dependent on the data given by us.

II. Processing of Collected Data: Data processing is one type of system and each system should have a purpose. Hence different types of processing are required for different types of systems to serve the purpose of that particular type of data processing system. Basically, it is the core part of the system because without it nothing can be done. Data alone cannot provide useful information. Without processing the entire data processing system is useless. If seen, a computer system is used only for processing and today what we are writing or remains a part of any subject, it is due to processing because if it is not possible to do processing with a computer then today we would not be writing here and you are not reading. Processing is the main function of the computer. It is used only for processing. Although a variety of programs are used to perform this task because the computer or processor cannot do the processing on its own, it requires a program to develop the same kind of application program that it needs. And the desired result is achieved with the help of the computer's processor.

III. Output or Result Basically the main purpose of using a data processor is to get the result or find the output in the desired format. For any system its objective is the most important, the whole system is designed to achieve the objective, if the objective is not achieved, the whole system fails, no matter how much time is given in it has gone or hard work has been done, if the desired result is not achieved, the whole system is considered useless, hence the very important place of output for the user or the customer or any business organization or any organization that uses that data processing system.

For example, if a person uses a washing machine to wash clothes and if he does not get the washed clothes, then the whole washing machine is useless or the juicer does not get the fruit juice, then the juicer is useless.

If seen, only output remains at the end of any system, collecting data, processing, all this is left behind. Whatever data processing system is used, it works on a predefined program basis as data processors not only do the processing of data but also have to prepare it in a particular format. Because many time we get results in the form of charts. Sometimes it is needed in the form of tables, sometimes it is needed in the form of graphs, in this way the data processor software also converts the processed data into the desired format.

1. Principles of Data Processing

There are some basic principles of data processing. Although data processing is a normal process of a computer, to know why we are given so much attention to it or in today's many business organizations, offices, banks, colleges, industries, financial institutions, etc., we need to know some of its basic principles. We need to know that because of the principle of data processing, we attach so much importance to it, in fact, the act of data processing is all the applications of computer programs like DBMS, word processor, spreadsheet, PowerPoint presentation, paintbrush, etc., sound editing, sound processors, multimedia players, web browsers and even a normal text editor also do the same job of data processing, so what is the reason why we are studying only data processing separately or it has given a different place? Why do some programs fall under the category of data processors only? Like Hadoop, HPCC, Statwing, etc. So let's know about some basic principles of data processing, after that you will understand yourself what is the importance of data processing tools in today's era?

1. **Single Fact Countless Meanings**

This is the first and very basic of data processing. Basically, the whole theory of data processing is based on this principle. We can also say that data processing is born from this principle. So let's know this very interesting principle of data processing which has changed the world especially the way of doing business.

Data processing considers this as its principle, innumerable meanings of the same fact can be deduced, the amount of processing power it can deduce as much as that fact and there is no need to tell how much is the processing speed of the computer? Computers were used to extract the meaning of facts. it is not that before the computer, the work of data processing was not done or this principle is a new theory. This principle is also old. Data processing is also old, but due to a lack of human capacity for processing, the available data could not be used as effectively as it could be done with the help of a computer.

We can understand this principle very clearly with the help of an example, suppose there is a fact

"Mohan goes to college every morning at 10:00 AM."

Now, this single fact can be deduced innumerable meanings. A sound surprising but it is true. It is up to the processing person what he can deduce from it. Like Mohan goes to college every morning at 10:00 it means that he studies in college. His age is not mentioned anywhere in the statement but since he goes to college, his age may be between 20 to 30 years. Because he goes to college every day, so he will be healthy. He goes to college means he is an intermediate pass out; the name is Mohan, which means he is a Hindu.

These are some common result finding things; such things are often seen in spy films or read in spy books, this theory is so effective that it is mostly used in intelligence services. On the basis of this principle, such things are detected which cannot be known in general, this process is also called data analysis, the deeper the data analysis; the more different results can be detected. It can be said that no more information can be extracted from those available data. Extracting more and more information from the available data depends on how many different methods of processing the data we use. It depends on the attitude of the processor of the data, how he sees the available facts or data. A simple event, a simple statement, becomes very important to the person processing a piece of simple information. Principles of Data Processing Whereas it is only dependent on that countless information can be obtained from a single fact, then imagine today when many facts are collected through the Internet, then how much information can be extracted from it, then one concludes that data processing the area is limitless. Any business establishment, any organization can grow maximum by using data processing because there is no limit to development, in the same way, there is no limit to data processing, that is why there is a very wide opportunity for data processing in a business organization.

2. **Information's are interrelated** Most of the time it happens that we have a lot of information but we can't find the desired result. But when we try to connect all information to each other they produce more valuable and desirable information.

Sometimes it seems that there is no relation between any two information, but if the relationship is searched properly or deeply, it is often seen which events are related in this way it has become a theory that All events are directly or indirectly related to some way or the other, it also depends on the processing, the more powerful our processing capacity, the more we can detect the relationship of information and the more we can. The more information we explore, the more we can get useful information. Because data processing has a purpose, it is not that processing happens only once. Information can be extracted again from proceed output and used for processing. The process continues till we get the result which we were looking for. For example, in a detective film, a detective continues to investigate until he finds the culprit and collects and processes all kinds of information to find the culprit. Some information is received, then it relates that information to each other, then some information comes out, then it is the task of the detective to extract the desired information from all those information. What is the difference between a normal person and a detective? The detective also sees the same ordinary events or information but has a different point of view, he extracts them from ordinary events and information in different ways that ordinary people cannot do in the same way. In this way, what is the difference between a general detective and a very specialized detective, a very specialized detective also does fact-finding like a normal detective but his processing power is different, he processes the information from a different perspective and gives new results.

3. **More data more accuracy** As much as data has to be collected for processing, the accuracy level of the result will be higher.

The more you have the data sample, the more correct conclusion you will be able to draw. You have ever wondered why the whole world believes that every person who is alive must die one day, even it is said that this is the world's biggest truth. No one can deny it. How did this greatest truth come to be known? What is going to happen in the future, that is, how all the people will die one day, what was the technology behind it or which algorithm was used, the answer to this question is very simple, that is, more and more data samples. We have found this data from our history till date and not a single exception of which has not been found till date that: a person has not died.

This strengthened our faith even more. In the beginning, one may not believe that every person will die, but gradually when more and more data started being received, then this belief of the people became absolutely firm. It can also be understood with an example, sometimes we do not believe something to be true, but when we hear the same thing from many people, then we start believing it to be true, as is often the case in the case of rumor, but then sometimes there is a rumor. Of course, once the mind considers it to be true because it is the principle that whenever we hear the same thing over and over again from different people, we start believing it to be true. And this is also a principle of processing, the more data we get from different places, its reliability goes on increasing.

Suppose we have a fact that "Ajay is an honest person" it may not be as reliable as it got from one place but if we get to know this fact from different sources from different programs from different people then we will start relying more on this fact. This principle is also used in data processing because often not only one algorithm is used in processing facts, but fact analysis is done with the help of many different algorithms. So that the same By matching the results among themselves, it can be trusted that the result that has come is accurate, that is why data analysis and data processing software focus on collecting data as much as possible.

4. **The future can be predicted not exactly but most of it**

If the available data is analyzed and processed properly, then we cannot make accurate predictions of the future, but we can make a rough idea of the future. For example, if an old man is very seriously ill from an incurable disease, we cannot tell the exact date and time of his death, but we can definitely estimate that he will not live for very long. If seen, the ultimate objective of data processing is future prediction. Many times the result of exit polls comes before the election in the news, it is an example of data processing, nowadays it is often seen that exit polls are correct. After all, how do they make it without real results, it is the wonder of data processing. The data processing software that is there today, in the future, when it is in its most advanced stage, then surely many future predictions can be done accurately. some examples of this so it is also seen in today's applications, such as the suggestion video of YouTube, it analyzes the data of our previous history and sends it to the suggestion video and it is often seen that it is of our choice, so how can that program know our mind? And he is not an introvert, but it is a miracle of a data processing program. In the same way, the social media site gives friend suggestions on Facebook, it is also often seen that he suggests to the person that he is connected to us, many times it happens that we have forgotten them but the data which is on Facebook is analyzed. After processing, the Facebook program does some fact-finding and gives us some friend suggestions based on that. The purpose of any data processing software is not only to provide design and output by processing but also to do fact-finding. Nowadays much data processing software comes which after collecting the data; find the facts in different ways than themselves. Then by converting them back into input data, again they find out new facts from them. That is the main advantage of technology that you can find the fact that is not entered into the system

8.4 Methods of data processing

Manual

In manual mode all the work related to processing of data is done without any machine or mechanical equipment. Meaning that this method is completely human based, in this, humans use their own intelligence to process the data and find out the result. For example we use copy pen to write something and with the help of that some calculations etc Even if it comes under manual data processing.

Mechanical

In the mechanical method, some small devices are used for processing data, such as the abacus device was used for addition, subtraction, etc. In the early times, typewriters were used to type documents; that is an example of mechanical devices. We can consider it under mechanical data processing. Any such equipment which is running without electricity should be considered under mechanical data processing. It is very less powerful than electronic but sometimes it also proves to be very useful due to its simplicity.

Electronic / digital / software

Generally, the data processing we talk about is digital data processing. Mainly it is the data processing: we are talking about. The process of data processing is done with the help of computer and which does data processing with the help of application program. Digital data processing is computer based but at the same time it is also computer program based because computer cannot run without program. Data processing today comes in the category of a complex program, so we can also call it software data processing.

8.5 Steps of Data Processing

1. Data collection this is the first and primary step that should be taken before any other steps. In this step, many kinds of data collection methodology such as interviews, focus group discussions, observation, photography, video, surveys, questionnaires, and case studies are used to collect data. These methodologies are generally performed in offline mode (on paper) after that it is entered into the computer system for further processing. There is some other online sources are also be used to collect data such as social media platform, online feedback form, online survey form, web survey chat, online focus group, usage data, etc.

Whatever tool or methodology is used for data collection, the objective should be to collect data as much as possible and from different types of sources. In data collection, it should also be taken care that the data is correct and reliable because the whole further process is dependent on it. If it is wrong then the result will also be wrong.

So it is very important to keep care of what kind of techniques or tools are used to collect data. a standard tool or technique must be used to find fruitful outcomes in the data processing process.

Note: xml, csv, doc, xls etc. are some common file format for Data collection.

2. Data storage

The most important function after data collection is to store the data. It is an intermediary stage of data processing between the Collection of data and the rest of the steps of data processing. It is like a buffer between data collection and the rests part of a data processing system.

The next step of data processing is to store the data because, in order for the data to be processed, it is necessary to store it first because data collection is a diverse step; it consists of many types of elements, many types of tools, many types of application programs. It works on both offline and online modes. It first collects all the different types of data received from different places at one place, so that the further stages of data processing get the data from one place. It is like a warehouse, the way in which different types of goods from different cities are collected in the warehouse in one place, in the same way, the data processing system also works for the storage of data in this stage.

Sometimes it also happens that the data is on paper or in the form of images or in the form of voice. Many times the data is also in unstructured form, in which case the data has to be converted into digital format first, so this work is also done under the data storage step.

Obviously, there is a requirement of a huge amount of data storage devices for this because the application programs doing the work of data processing do not solve the problem of storage, there is a requirement of different types of devices for storage. Some common devices for data storage like CDs, DVDs, and hard disks are used but they are not capable of storing huge amounts of data. Different types of storage systems are used to store a large-scale amount of data. Whichever storage device is used, it should be kept in mind that it can store a large amount of data, as well as the transfer speed of the storage device is also fast and the potential for data loss is negligible.

Following are some examples of storage solutions that can meet the data processing system requirement.

- Solid-State Drives (SSDs)
- Cloud storage
- Redundant array of independent disks (RAID)

3. Data arrangement

It is an immediately step after data storage and before data processing. The data has to be arranged according to the requirement of the application program. In this process, the data also has to be filtered because many times unwanted, undesirable or such data comes in the data collection which is of no importance. Therefore, in these circumstances, it is appropriate to filter such data because better work of processing will be done on the basis of effective data not too much unnecessary data. Affect the work, so along with arranging the data at this step, they also need to be filtered, this work is sometimes done with the help of a separate application program or mostly the application program from which the data processing work is done. The work of sorting and filtering is also done from the same application program; there are different algorithms for sorting and filtering, with the help of which this work is done.

For example, suppose at the time of data collection, we got data in three different languages. At the time of data collection, we do not care in which language or what type of data it is, we only store it in one place but if the program of data processing requires data in a certain format, then first of all it is necessary that the data should be arranged according to the requirement of that program, as if a data program can process English words, then we can use only data that are in the English language from the collection of data. Sometimes there are some programs that perform the operation on sorted numbers like the program of binary search, this program depends on the fact that the numbers which are input to arrange them are in sorted form. be in order from smallest to largest. In this way, we see that there are different types of programs that have to give data in a particular order. Keeping this in mind, this step is needed.

Following are some popular sorting programs used to arrange the data in ascending or descending order

- Insertion Sort.
- Selection Sort.
- Quick Sort.
- Bubble Sort.
- Heap Sort.
- Radix Sort.
- Bucket Sort.
- Merge Sort

4. Data processing it is a core unit of the whole data processing system. it is a set of very complex programs which is used to achieve the goal for which the whole data processing system is developed. It is like the engine of any motor car. Every data processing system has its own purpose and to achieve that particular purpose, whatever operation a particular application program performs, is in this phase Such as verifying data, a transformation of data, organization of data, integration of data, and extraction of data. This is the most secret part of the data processing system because different software has their own different techniques different methods different algorithm to find out the result.

Following are some popular advanced data processing software

HADOOP

HPCC

Storm

Qubole

Cassandra

5. Data analysis. This is the next step of data processing. After processing an intermediate output is produced which we cannot call the result but we can definitely call it intermediate result, we can also call it raw result i.e. raw output because data analysis is yet to be done on the basis of this result. Basically, data analysis uses all kinds of processing but using different aspects. This is the same part that works differently in every software The better the analysis power of the software, the better it's quality and the more useful that software will be considered.

As we know from the theory of data processing that a single fact can have multiple meanings. New results also generate new facts and on the basis of this, re-analysis is done. This process continues till the purpose for which the data is being processed is not achieved. Nowadays word processor software uses it. When the user keeps on typing the sentence while typing, then data processing and data analysis both keep working, based on the importance given by the user, he matches the word so that he can also correct the wrong word typed by the user.

Following are some popular data analytics tool

1. Excel
2. Tableau Public:
3.Python
4. SAS:
5. Apache Spark
6. R Programming
7. RapidMiner:
8. KNIME
9. QlikView
10. Splunk:

6. Data presentation. This is the last step of data processing. Ultimately result or outcome of all processing tasks is ready after the data analysis step.

But as we know that the output of the computer is machine-based, it has to be converted into multiple forms because the output is useless until the human being understands. Because all these processes is being done for the human, so the output must be changed in such a format that it can be easily understood by the human being. Output result formatting is the work of this step. In this step, the data or the output that we have got is displayed with the help of various formats of presentation such as text file, excel file, chart, or graph. It mostly depends on the requirement of the application program sometimes more than one software's is also used for this task because many times it happens that the data processing tool we use to present the output is not appropriate. If it happens, the help of any other software can also be taken. Following are some popular formats for output presentation

Plain text file

Table

Graph

Chart

Image file

Maps or vector

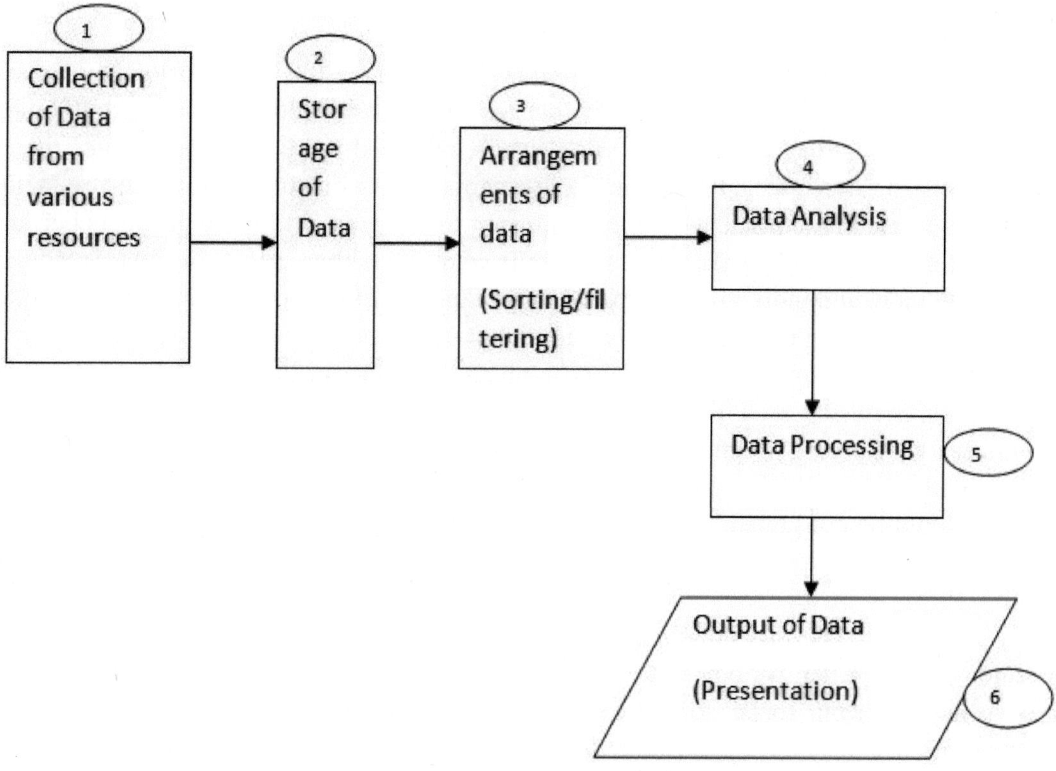

Fig: Steps of data processing

8.6 Advance Data Processing Technology

In data processing, the same fact has to be analyzed repeatedly from different angles from different perspectives, this is a complex task and requires a lot of storage and processing speed and we know that human capacity is limited. In the course of the gradual development of the computer, it was also thought that why such complex task should not be done with the help of a computer. A computer can perform this type of activity speedily and automatically. Many new technologies were developed for this because the old program was not able to do such a challenging task. Data processing tools are being used in many business applications. It is being used very successfully in many fields, even in word processor's typing to check spelling, in voice recording, in voice typing, in YouTube's video suggestions, in Google's search engine, in weather forecasting, etc. we should Know about some of the most important new technologies of data processing.

First of all, a machine was made for some simple tasks like adding and subtracting, which is called a calculator. After that, the needs and aspirations of man increased. Logical work was also started to be done by machine. For which the computer was invented. After becoming a computer, there was a gradual development in it and it kept on achieving new achievements, now along with addition or subtraction or simple logic, many more complex tasks are performed by the computer. Nowadays, some such analytical work, which used to be the identity of a very intelligent man, is done by computer, which is called Artificial Intelligence. It is a form of gradual development of the computer itself. Today, the work that computers used to do with the help of programs only, more focus is being given on getting those tasks performed automatically and it is very similar to human beings, hence it is named Artificial Intelligence. Processing should also be done automatically, so some new advanced technology is available and they are as follows

8.7 Role of Data Processing system in Business organization

The most basic objective of any business organization is to earn maximum profit; this profit mainly depends on two things, the cost of the goods or services and the sale price.

Profit = sale price - cost price

In order to maximize profit, one must reduce the cost as well as increase the selling price. But we see that there is a limit to reduce the cost and increase the selling price because if the cost is reduced too much if done, the quality of the goods or services will be affected and if the sale price is increased more than the sales of the goods in the competitive market can also be affected. So for any business organization to maximize profit, cost reduction and sales can be done. With the increase in the price, it is more important to sell more and more products because if there is a profit of ? 2 on a unit, then it is obvious that the more units sold, the higher the profit. That is why any business organization wants to sell more and more product units. The production of the commodity is not a big deal, but how to sell it is a big problem because the more the item is sold, the more the profit will increase.

There is no limit to profit maximization because how much an item can be sold is not generally known, for example, in the early days, television used to be a combination of several households in a single house, after that the TV reached every house over a period of time. With the passage of time, there were two or three TVs in every house. The same situation is with mobile phones and many other things, today's society is a consumerist society. In this, more and more items would be consumed, which provides a golden opportunity for any business organization. In order to sell the product as much as possible, not only it is necessary to sell the item, but it is also necessary to create the need of the item.

When do we buy something? The answer is when we need that item. So the need has to be created for the product to be sold. Many times it is seen that we buy something just because it is a status symbol or it is necessary for our identity, for our personality, for our social existence. We see that buying or selling of the item It depends on many factors and while the profit of a business organization depends only on selling more and more of the commodity, then in this situation it is also necessary to strategize different ways to sell the commodity because only the traditional methods of the commodity It is not possible to sell such a large quantity.

Today's era is the age of the Internet; today's market is completely dependent on the Internet, many businesses, many companies, many business organizations, use e-commerce. And even some companies do their entire business through e-commerce only. Today the scope of the market is very wide for any business organization. It is not so easy for any business organization to sell goods in a competitive market. As the market gets bigger, the competition is also bigger because if any business organization will make any delay or mistake in the website process, then the customer will immediately switch to another platform because now he does not have to go anywhere physically to change the shop to change the platform, only he has to open a new website from his computer or click with the mouse.

In view of such circumstances, in today's date, if any business organization wants to get maximum profit, then it will have to take the help of data processing because today's entire market is based on computers, the internet, mobile phone, electronic gadgets, Social media or website, etc.

If a business organization wants to sell a product, then it has to show it on the website, then a customer reaches its website, reads its details, sees its image, that is, both the buyer and the seller do not interact directly. In between, only the website is the medium. The more attractive and effective we present our item, the higher the chances of selling it. The website has an important place and if not the content data of the website then what else? In this way, the importance of data cannot be ignored in the world of e-commerce. At the same time, one thing cannot be denied that if the processing of that data will not be done effectively then it may not provide us as much profit as is expected.

Whereas today the whole business through computer or internet. In this, the source of data comes from different types of sources, so synchronization of data between those different sources is also necessary and there are many types of complex tasks which are not possible without data processing software, So if any business organization is eager for progress, growth, maximum profit, then it must definitely use software like data processor, otherwise, it will be left far behind in this online market.

Let us understand it better with the help of different points. That is how data processing is done for any business organization. How it helps in achieving the basic objective profit maximization

Target customer: Target customer means searching for those customers from a very large customer group who are eligible for your goods or services. such as if a company Sells small children's toys, then its customers will be parents of young children or a person who is related to young children, a small child cannot himself be a target customer for that product because he is not able to buy the item or assume Suppose a company makes umbrellas, then it will target the customers of those places where it rains more.

Targeting or selecting a customer becomes very easy with the help of data processing software because the Internet's data is carried by the users of the Internet. Then today we use any website, then it first takes our data from us like our name, mobile number, email id, etc. Today mobile phones are also linked to our email IDs. Today email ID has become our identity and with the help of this email ID, the data of many customers reach the website. The data of the target customers which must be for a particular company or a particular product can be easily filtered. Today many well-known search engines or social media websites do this work; they have a lot of user data that can be used in e-commerce based businesses. The company does this in abundance.

It can be understood with the help of an example. Suppose on XYZ website, 1000000 users have registered themselves then thereof on that website, that 1000000 will be data users .1000000 users will be of a different name, space, form, age and income group, everyone's choice will be different, everyone's interest will be different. Everyone's life will be different. Now suppose that a company If wants to sell the car contacts the website XYZ and asks for the data of such customers who will be in the income group required to buy the car as well as those who will be interested in driving, today this thing is very much with the help of the website. It can be easily found out who is interested in whom, because if you search something from the Internet, then that search company stores this data, what are we searching for searching our interests from the history and needs, can be traced. This data is very useful for any company. Based on this data, they target the customer. So XYZ The website will give that data in the form of output by processing the data to the new company who would be willing to buy the car. In this way, it will be easy to sell the car to that company because it has the data of such users who actually want to buy the car. In this way, we see that data processing helps in targeting the customer.

Effective marketing: To sell an item or service, it has to be marketed first. Advertising has to be done so that more and more people come to know about that product or service. In traditional marketing techniques or traditional advertising techniques, the target audience was not used; only newspapers, hoardings, television channels, etc. were used. Promoted was not done with the help of the target audience. With the help of data processing technology, any company can advertise. Advertisement is only among those audiences who are related to it. In this case, only selected users will be given information about those items who will be willing to buy those items Or about the service they really want to receive. The biggest example of this is seen in websites; today different types of advertisements come on different websites for different users. It is often seen that a person who is interested in the field gets to see the advertisements of his interest on the website; this is due to data processing. The websites on which we navigate or download or about which search engines ask questions, all these data are collected and selected with the help of data processing tools, target areas are selected. In this way, data processing contributes a lot to effective marketing.

We can understand this with the help of an example. Suppose you search for the price of a car on a website. Compare prices of different types of cars. This data reaches the servers of the search engine, and then the search engine company gets the information that you are interested in buying the car. Now the company selling the car gets this data from the search engine company. Now whatever website you go to, you will get to see the advertisement of the car of that company it may happen that someone else has gone to the same page and he/she may get to see the advertisement of any other item of the other company due to data processing. Cause happens. Search engine servers contain a huge amount of data and this data is very valuable to the company. Today's entire market is dependent on this data; so many companies provide many facilities for free so that they can get our data like our name, age, address, educational qualification, income, mobile number, family details, friend details, etc. After collecting this data and processing the information, information is extracted that helps them to sell their goods or services.

Market Analysis If a business organization goes to start any new production work, first of all, it does market analysis. Two things have an important place in market analysis, first is the product that a company is going to produce, whether there is a demand in the market or not? And if so, in what quantity can it be sold? And second, how is the market situation? Many times it happens that there is a demand for the commodity, but the condition of the customer is not such that he can buy the item. Therefore analysis of the overall market is also necessary. In its absence, sometimes the entire production is wasted. Does market analysis also include some other things like where will the product be sold? What will be its cost? As long as such products remain in the market. will they be useful or not? Is there any other alternative to that product in the market or not? Should there be an offer with that product etc? Several types of analysis are required before a product can be made. All these data-related work can be done easily with the help of data processing software, so data processing is very important in any business organization and especially in today's online market, it cannot be ignored at all.

Finance: The finance sector is considered to be a very sensitive area for any company because the basic objective of any business organization is to earn a profit, that is, it is a matter of finance. If the work of this department does not run smoothly or there is any disturbance in this department. It will have a direct impact on the financial condition of the business organization or in other words we can say that if the finance sector is further strengthened then it will prove to be very effective in strengthening any business organization. It is completely dependent on the data; it contains very important data such as the price of the product, the cost of the item, the account of various types of transactions in a particular period, the loan taken by the company.

A lot of data is related to finance fields, so not only computers but also computers require a special programming technique, which is made only for a field like finance. There are many tools for data processing that are related to financial data analysis and which can do it in a much better way.

There are times when financial data shows that the company has made a profit but it is also possible that this is actually wrong. This type of error cannot be caught by any normal application. This requires specialized data processor tools, which can examine the same data in greater depth. Particularly it is used in large organizations to detect such types of deficiencies which cannot be done by the common person or by a normal computer program. Data processing software tool is a fast tool for the financial sector which is certainly nothing less than a boon for any business organization.

HR management: No matter how much development happens in technology, no matter how much work is performed automatically or no matter how much a business uses technology, but the importance of human resources can never be underestimated.

There are many such decisions or there are many such tasks that are possible only by human beings. That is why human resources have an incomparable place in any business organization. No matter how advanced technology is used in a company, but if the employees working in it will not be honest, hardworking, and reliable then that company can never develop. Therefore, it is very important for any company to have a quality HR section. The data processing system also contributes to the improvement of human resources. Any business organization can select the most suitable candidate with the help of data processing tools at the time of recruitment of employees. Today, if you want to know about a person, you must find out about his social media platforms, information related to his phone's data bank, website search history, etc. If you do this, then many things can be found out about the person that usually cannot be detected by the traditional methods of interview. Like about his nature, about his merits and demerits, about his character, etc.

Today, many business organizations opt for data processing at the time of interview. With the help of data processing, that organization can get qualified honest reliable employees and there is no need to tell that how much growth that organization can grow if a business organization is fully equipped with qualified, honest, hardworking, and reliable employees.

Report making: In different types of business organizations, there is a need to generate multiple types of reports based on day-to-day activities so that many types of transactions or presentations of many types of information can be done easily. We know how data processing tools can effectively do the work of report making with the help of graph table chart etc.

The processing tool helps a lot in doing paperwork; today almost all the big business organizations have realized the paperless office. Today almost all office work is done through a computer-assisted data processing medium as it increases the speed and also increases the accuracy of the work. The chances of making a mistake are also negligible.

In short, we can say that data processing can be done by any business organization. Every area of any business organization is directly or indirectly related to data processing software, the more use of this tool, the more it will provide benefits. Today if a business organization neglects important tools like data processing then it can never make its mark on the global level because today's era is the era of the global market and for the global market one has to take the help of online tools. It is impossible to survive without data processing in the online market.

8.8 Data Management

Data management is the process of preparing the data for any specific reason. The basic purpose of data management is to keep data in such a way that it can be accessed, readable, and extractable by any other further process.

Collection of data, security of data, sorting of data, filtering of data, simplification of data are some common functions of data management. DBMS itself is an example of a data management tool. We can include any software, device, service, or system in the data management group if they perform data management-related processes. like we can say ms-Access is a data management software because it performs a lot of data management-related tasks such as storing the data, sorting data, filtering the data, creating the database, updating the database, delete the database, maintaining relations between tables. But we cannot say any word processor software as a data management tool. It can be said that it is a data processor but not data management.

Difference between data management and data processor

Data management focuses more on data acquisition and preparation for other purposes in the organization. The main tasks in the "Data Management" area include creating databases, uploading data to these data stores, backing up files and creating historical copies, and "allowing" others in the organization to access certain data files and perhaps access those files. Additionally, it includes some rows and/or columns.

Data processing, essentially, "what value/information can we get from the data"? Processing, broadly speaking, is the application of "mathematical operations" to data. These include basic counting tasks such as generating summary counts of "events", creating reports with summary descriptive statistics and applying "data visualization" tools to create graphics that express the "information" in your data. "Processing" also includes the application of statistical modeling tools to predict future events based on historical data, to "cluster" or otherwise group similar units of analysis into separate groups, or to group the effectiveness of marketing campaigns and customer behavior but to assess similar "interference".

It can be said that the outcome of a data management system is the input of a data processing system.

The result of data management is the start of data processing. Data management creates a ground on which data processing building can stand.

Exercises

Objective type question

Choose the correct answer for the followings

1. The basic purpose of any data processing toll is to find the

(a) Formatted data (b) useful information (c) more data (d)formatted output

2. Which of the following statement is true about the data processing system?

(a) Single program is not sufficient to perform all data processing tasks

(b) It can be done using many programs

(c) Data analysis is a part of data processing

(d) all of the above

3. Processing means to perform

(a) Set of actions to get a useful result

(b) Many tasks simultaneously

(c) step by step action

(d) a big task

4. Redundant array of independent disks (RAID) is a

(a) data processing tool (b) data input tool (c) data storage tool (d) none of these

5. Insertion sort, quick sort, and bubble sort are some examples of

(a) Data collection techniques (b) Algorithm used in data arrangement (c) Data filtering techniques (d) all of these

6. Which of the following is a popular tool used for BigData processing?

(a) ms-access (b) ms-excel (c) quick-access (d) Hadoop

7. HPCC is a ______________

(a) data processing tool (b) data input tool (c) data storage tool (d) none of these

8. Which of the following would be the first thing you would do to do the task of data Processing step by step?

(a) Data collection (b) data arrangement (c) data processing (d) data presentation

9. Where does the place of graph table or chart come in the phased action plan of data Processing?

(a) Data collection (b) Data arrangement (c) Data processing (d) Data presentation

10. What is the ultimate goal of using a data processing system in any business organization?

(a) For better data management (b) Profit maximization

(c) Sale price comparison (d) Cost cutting

Theoretical questions

1. What do mean by data processing? Explain various steps involve in the processing of data.
2. Discuss the importance of a data processing system in any business organization.
3. Show how data processing is helpful in the decision-making process.
4. Describe the role of data processing to face the modern challenges of any business organization.
5. Write a short note on BigData, Data mining, and Data warehousing.
6. with the help of examples Explain different data processing methods.
7. Differentiates between data management and data processing system.

CHAPTER NINE

DATA AND FILE ORGANIZATION

9.1Data hierarchy The term Data hierarchy means the systematic organization of data. It refers to the proper and systematic grouping of data into many parts. With the help of a data hierarchy, we can categorize our data into various standard groups.

Here we will mainly learn about the hierarchy of data storage. Under the hierarchy of data storage, we move from the smallest unit of data storage to the largest unit. It should be thought of as something like a tree view. Like there is a hierarchy of posts in a company. such as a clerk works in a company, a supervisor does the job of supervising many clerks, many supervisors work under a single in-charge, many in charge work under the manager, many managers work under the biggest manager of a company under the general manager. In this way, there is a hierarchy of the posts of the company.

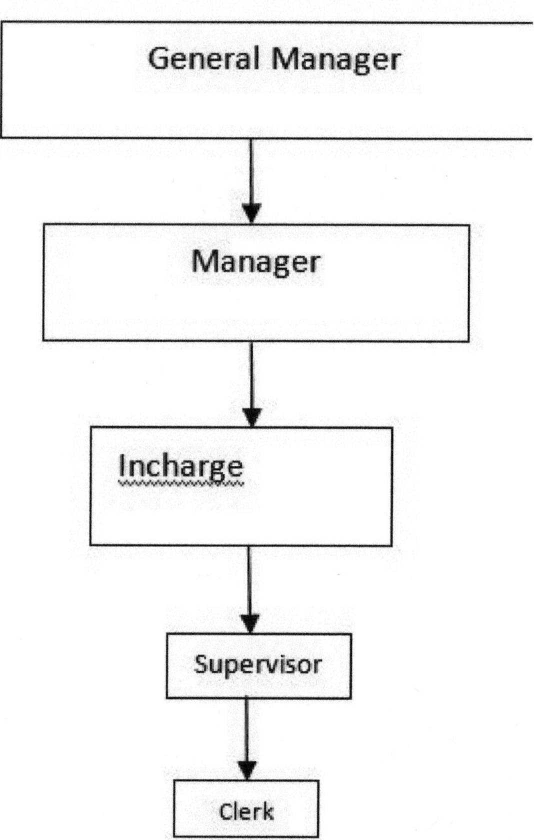

This type of hierarchy system is also applicable in data storage where there are many different groups of data storage and they also have a hierarchy. Let us understand the hierarchy of data storage.

The smallest unit of data storage is a character, many characters together form a field, and many fields together are called records. Similarly, many records together are called files and many files together form a database.

Therefore, the largest unit of data storage is the database. A database consists of many files. Each file is a collection of several records. Every record is a group of many fields and each field is formed with the help of characters. It can be better understood through the following.

character	character	character	character
Field			
Field	Field	Field	Field
Record			
Record	Record	Record	Record
File			
File	File	File	File
Database			

Character: This is the basic building block of data. It includes alphabets (a,b,c.........A,B,C.....),numbers(0,1,2,....),special symbols (@, #,$,%,......). it is the smallest unit of any data.

Field: A meaningful group of related characters is called field. In the given table example roll number, name, father's name, date of birth, city are some fields.

Record: A meaningful group of related fields.

When many fields are related to the same person, organization, or object, then the combination of all those fields is called a record. In a general sense, the meaning of the record is taken from the value of the fields such as in the given example Roll Number, Name, Fathers Name, Date of Birth, City are all these fields. But they are basically not called records until a value is inserted into them. But yes the combination of all of these, the group of all of these, the collection of all of these, the set of all of these can be called a record.

For example, in the table named Student Basic Information, the first entry in the column of roll number is 2110001, the first entry in the field of name is Ajay Kumar, in the father's name, Neelkanth Kumar, in the date of birth 12/5/2001, City Varanasi, all these records are in any way. Only one person is related to Ajay Kumar, thus we can say that the first row of this table is the record of Ajay Kumar because a record contains many fields; so many fields related to Ajay Kumar are also given here. Similarly, the second row pertains to the record of Vikas Yadav. In the given example there are a total of 9 such records.

File: A meaningful group of related records is called a file.

Many such records that belong to the same group are called files. As in the given example, there are 9 different records but all of them belong to the same group i.e. basic information of the student. So we can call it a file. Whose name is Student Basic Record? In the given example, a file named Student Basic Record is created by combining a total of 9 records of different students like Ajay Kumar, Vikas Yadav, Sunil Singh, etc.

Database: A set of integrated and related files is called a database.

In very general terms, a database is a set of many different interrelated files. The given example shows three files. These three files can be combinedly called a database. But it is to be especially noted that all the files, despite being different, should also be related to each other. It is not that one file is related to the student, the other file is related to the employee and by combining these two, we can say that it is a database. There will be many files related to the student itself, and then we can call them databases by combining them. All of them also need to have a relationship with each other. The second file is related to the student's current record. The student is the same as Ajay Kumar, Vikas Yadav, Sunil Singh, etc but the second file contains other records related to them like current year, subject stream, and previous result i.e. from the current record of the student. In this table students related other information like in which year he is studying at present? Which stream is he a student of? And what was his last result? Did he pass or fail? , are stored. This file is second but it pertains to the same students whose record was in the Student Basic Record in File One. That is, in this, we get information related to Ajay Kumar, Vikas Yadav, Sunil Singh, etc. In this sequence, we see that there are also three student qualifying exam records, except for the column of roll number, there are different fields like qualifying exam, Subject Stream, Marks Obtained, Total Marks. In this also there is other information of the same student. In file 3, the information related to the exam of Ajay Kumar, Vikas Yadav, Sunil Singh, etc. has been given, in this way we see that three files are related to a certain person even though they are different, that is, all the tables are related to each other. Therefore, we can call a group of these three files a database.

Example

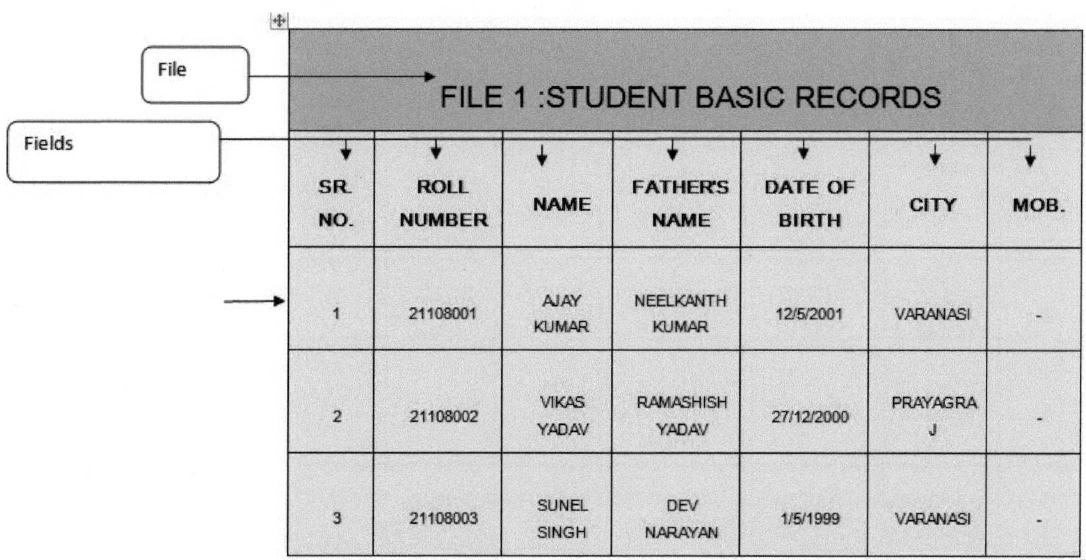

FILE 1 :STUDENT BASIC RECORDS						
SR. NO.	ROLL NUMBER	NAME	FATHER'S NAME	DATE OF BIRTH	CITY	MOB.
1	21108001	AJAY KUMAR	NEELKANTH KUMAR	12/5/2001	VARANASI	-
2	21108002	VIKAS YADAV	RAMASHISH YADAV	27/12/2000	PRAYAGRA J	-
3	21108003	SUNEL SINGH	DEV NARAYAN	1/5/1999	VARANASI	-

Records / Fields values

4	21108004	MOH. ABDUL KHAN	NUR ABDUL	8/8/2002	BALLIA	-
5	21108005	KISHOR AWASHTI	RAJSHEKHAR AWASTHI	12/1/2001	AZAMGARH	-
6	21108006	ACHINTYA SINGHAL	BRIJMOHAN SINGHAL	29/09/2000	KANPUR	-
7	21108007	SHREYA GUPTA	KRISHNA GUPTA	28/05/2002	JAUNPUR	-
8	21108008	KESHAW PANDEY	DEEPAK PANDEY	3/6/2000	GAZIABAD	-
9	21108009	ROHAN VERMA	KAILASH VERMA	31/12/2002	VARANASI	-

FILE 2:STUDENT CURRENT RECORD					
SR. NO.	ROLL NUMBER	CURRENT YEAR	SUBJECT STREAM	PREVIOUS RESULT	
1	21108001	FIRST YEAR	COMMERCE	PASSED	
2	21108002	FIRST YEAR	COMMERCE	PASSED	
3	21108003	FIRST YEAR	COMMERCE	PASSED	
4	21108004	FIRST YEAR	COMMERCE		Fail
5	21108005	FIRST YEAR	COMMERCE	PASSED	
6	21108006	FIRST YEAR	COMMERCE	PASSED	
7	21108007	FIRST YEAR	COMMERCE	PASSED	
8	21108008	FIRST YEAR	COMMERCE	PASSED	
9	21108009	FIRST YEAR	COMMERCE	PASSED	

FILE 3:STUDENT QUALIFYING EXAM RECORD					
SR. NO.	ROLL NUMBER	QUALIFYING EXAM	SUBJECT STREAM	MARKS OBTAINED	TOTAL MARKS
1	21108001	10+2	COMMERCE	410	500
2	21108002	10+2	COMMERCE	425	500
3	21108003	10+2	COMMERCE	450	500
4	21108004	10+2	SCIENCE	880	1000
5	21108005	10+2	COMMERCE	390	500
6	21108006	10+2	COMMERCE	389	500
7	21108007	10+2	SCIENCE	890	1000
8	21108008	10+2	COMMERCE	405	500
9	21108009	10+2	COMMERCE	419	500

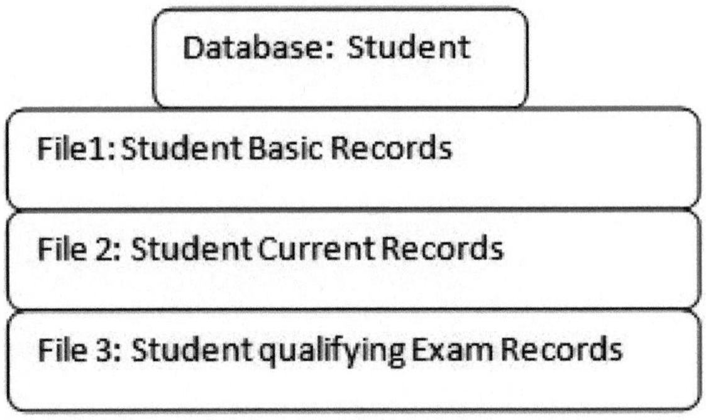

Database: Student

File1: Student Basic Records

File 2: Student Current Records

File 3: Student qualifying Exam Records

Enter Caption

9.2 Data File structure and organizations

Data file structures are the organization of data in secondary storage devices. This is basically used for minimizing the data access time and data storage space. Data representation and technique to access the data are two basic performance criteria of a file structure. On the basis of file structure permission, an application can read, write and modify the data.

A huge amount of different types of files are stored in the database and we know that there are many many records in the files, this number can be in 1000 to lakhs and even crores, so the question arises as to How to keep records of such a large quantity?

It is absolutely necessary to follow a specific methodology to organize access to and process such a huge amount of data. This method mainly depends on the demand of the application.

Mainly three methods are used for file organization Sequential, Direct, and Indexed sequential Out of these, which method should be used to organize the file depends on the application being used. Because different applications have different demands, different applications are made for different purposes, so it cannot be said that one method will work for every type of application. For a given application, that method will be most useful and beneficial; this meets the maximum demand of the application and is also economical. That is, save the time and money of the user using the application, as well as contribute fully to the maximum fulfillment of the purpose. Every file organization method has certain characteristics as well as some limitations. Before using any file organization method, the system designer must get proper information about their features and limitations, only then he can choose the right method.

The main purpose of file organization is to access the contents of the file. Whenever we talk about file organization, we talk about mass storage, that's why it becomes even more important. Different methods are used in computer science for how to access a particular data from a very large data set; the concept of key field is used in all methods whether it is a sequential method or a direct access method or an indexed sequential access method. To access any particular data, it is very important to have a key field. The way the primary key is used in the database management system (as in the given example 1 file 1, the field of roll number is the key field). The key field helps to access the data uniquely as any two students can have the same name but their roll number cannot be the same. Every record that is stored in the database must have a key field. The advantage of this key field is that whenever we have to search a record, instead of all the records, we only search the key field when that key. If the field is found, then all the records related to it can be accessed. As in the given table, if we want the details of Vikas Yadav, then instead of Vikas Yadav, we will search his data from his roll number 21108002, this makes it easy for both humans or machines to search the data. It is not that it is necessary to have a column of roll numbers in every table, but there must be one such field that is unique, the same unique field can be called key field. Our entire data file organization system depends on this field. There is a field of roll number in the student database because no two students can have the same roll number. In the same way, the account number of each customer in the bank is different; no two customers can have the same account number. Therefore, in the case of a bank, the account number can be called the key field. Thus, there must be different types of key fields in different data and files in different situations. In the case of a database management system, such a unique key field is also called the primary key.

So let us now know about those three file organization methods.

Sequential files

The file organization method is mainly concerned with storing, accessing, and processing data. The main question is which sequence should be used to store access and process the file, in which way we will access the data. Under this method, we access the record based on the key field, either increasing or decreasing sequentially, we process or store it. As the name of the sequential file access method is clear, it involves the importance of a sequence, that is, one after the other in a sequential manner.

For example, if 100 plates are to be kept on the dining table then definitely we will use the sequential file access method technique because we will place the plates one above the other i.e. use the sequential method to store the plate has done. At the same time, whenever we have to access those plates, we have to take them in a sequence i.e. in both cases we have to pay attention to the sequence to keep and use the plate. With the help of this method, 100 or 200 plates can easily be kept on a small table.

This method is also used to store/access the data on the disk. Under this method, the records are kept one after the other, the third after the second; the fourth after the third, and so on. The ordering of records is either in ascending order or descending order depending on the key field. The computer stores the data on the basis of its field as well as accesses it. Their order is determined on the basis of the key field itself.

Tape drive is an example of sequential file access. Audio cassettes were used to listen to songs in earlier times; they were an example of tape drives. In which the song was stored in the reel of the cassette. And with the help of a motor, the reel was rotated, as the reel moved forward, so did the song, the whole song could be played in one sequence respectively. If we want to listen to the song of the direct last, first we had to forward the cassette, if we want to listen to the beginning songs, then we had to rewind and reach back first, meaning that if we wanted to listen to a song immediately, then it was not possible. It was also a drawback of sequential file access

The technology of data storage or access also depends on the storage device. The storage device is manufactured keeping the access technology in mind. Storage media such as magnetic tape punched paper tape, punched cards, or magnetic disks are used to store, access data in a sequential manner. Meaning if we use these devices for data storage then it means our data will be stored and accessed in a sequence.

Advantages of sequential files

i. The logic of this technique is very simple. Put the data one after one. So it is very easy to organize, store, access, maintain and understand.

ii. Because of its simplicity its implementation is also very simple.

iii. There is no need for any separate address generation mechanism to store the data as in other methods of file organization.

iv. Devices which are used to store data are less costly compared to other devices which are based on other file organization mechanisms.

v. This technique is especially beneficial for those places where the data size is less because if the data size is large then it will take time to access the last data.

The disadvantage of sequential files

i. Such data which is, in the beginning, can be accessed quickly but if the data size is large then it takes more time to access the middle data or the last data. And if they are accessed again and again then even more time is wasted. Therefore, it may not be a useful file organization technique for places with frequent access to data.

ii. It is not useful in applications that require frequent access to data and updating them.

iii. If the sequence of data is disturbed anywhere in the middle, then the entire series gets disturbed, so there is a high risk of data damage in it.

iv. There is often the problem of data redundancy because different key fields are generated for different data and every new data is stored in a new location because it does not have any separate address generation scheme for data storage.

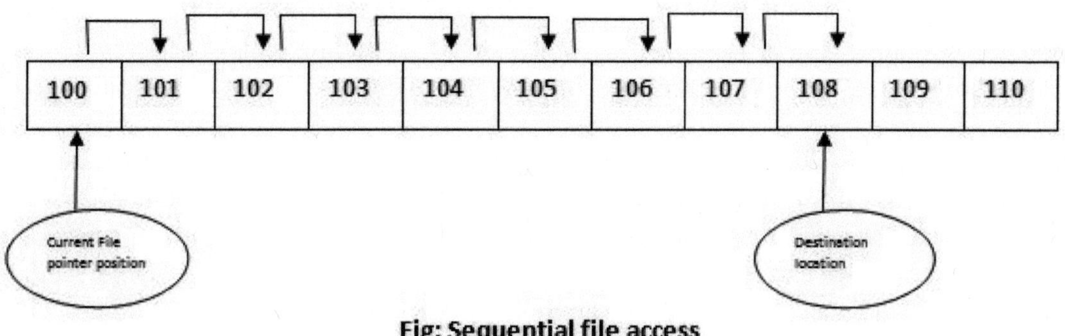

Fig: Sequential file access

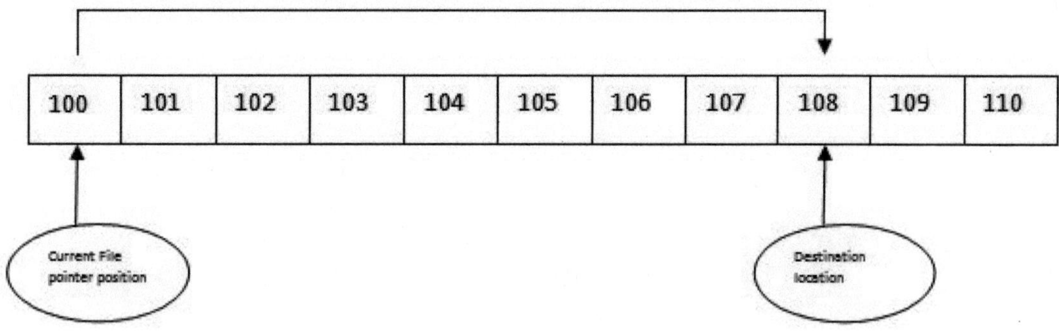

Fig: Direct access

Get the location from index table

Index table

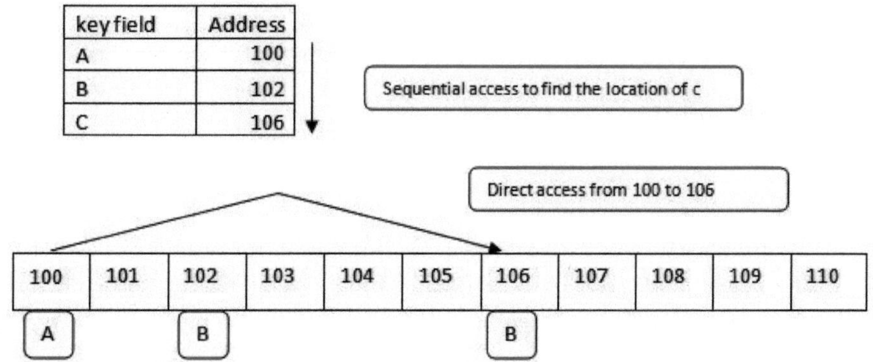

Fig: Indexed sequential access

Direct Files

In this type of file organization technique, data can be stored or accessed directly without following any sequence.

In this method, the operating system can store the data at any location on the disk or access it directly from any location. As this was not the case in the sequential file, the data had to be stored immediately after the previous start location.

For example, a table of plates placed on a dining table, when stacked one above the other, is an example of a sequential file access method. But if the same plate is placed side by side on the table, then neither we will need any sequence neither to place the plate nor to lift the plate, we can place the plate wherever we want and whatever plate is needed whenever we want. Yes, we can pick it up. Or if the glass of water is not kept on the table, then the sequential method will not work there, where we use the direct method, a glass full of water is placed on the table, there is no need to follow any sequence in which Anyone who wants to drink water can lift any glass from anywhere at any time.

CD or DVD drive is an example of a direct access method. In this, the operating system writes the data without following any sequence. Whatever data we want to access, we can access it directly. As in the old-fashioned audio cassettes it could not. We had to forward the entire cassette to listen to the song of the last, but if you are listening to the song from CD, then in that you can select and listen to the song of the last, so we can say that CD / DVD is an example of direct access whereas Old-fashioned audio cassettes are an example of sequential file access.

Any storage device is manufactured keeping in mind the file organization method.

As we know, the technology of data storage or access also depends on the storage device. The storage device is manufactured keeping the access technology in mind. Storage media such as drum, disk, and strip files store/access data directly.

That is, if we use these devices for data storage, it means that our data will be stored and accessed directly. No sequence is required in this technique.

Such storage devices which are based on direct file technology are called direct access storage devices (DASD) because it requires a special device mechanism. The DASD device is based on such technology so that the file can be directly accessed or stored. That is to say, it is not possible to do this with the help of a program alone.

This technique is more complicated than the sequential method. In this technique, a mathematical function called hashing is used to generate addresses that can be mapped from record key field address into DASD storage address. The address generating function is selected in such a way that the generated address should be evenly distributed over the entire range of the file area and a unique address should be generated for each record key.

Advantages of direct files

i. The biggest advantage of this technique is that it can store/access data at a very high speed as it does not follow any sequence.

ii. It is more helpful in applications where there is frequent data access.

iii. There is no hassle of putting the data in any order before processing

iv. This technique is very useful even for very large data size as it was not possible in Sequential

v. The time taken to access the data in the beginning or in the last or in the middle is the same, whereas it was not so in the sequential file system, in that the initial data used to be accessed quickly, the middle used to take more time and in the last Stored data queries took more time to store

vi. It is very effective in places like the airline, railway reservation system, etc. because it has to access the stored data frequently from different locations. Here the direct method is also necessary because it is a real-time system. Time is given top priority here

vii. Modern operating systems use virtual memory technology, in which data or files have to be repeatedly read from disk and stored back there (this technique is called swapping) in such a direct file method operating system absolutely necessary for this method.

The disadvantage of direct files

i. The Architecture and Technology of this Technique is Very Complicated. So it is not very easy to implement it.

ii. The operating system must also support this type of file system; otherwise, this technology will not work

iii. It requires a special type of storage device (DASD) which is also a bit costly.

iv. For applications where data is not accessed frequently, this technology is unusable or not very useful as these storage devices cost more than sequential storage devices.

v. It also has the overhead of address generation, so the operating system cannot store or access the data immediately after the user's command.

vi. The operating system has to do some processing only then it can access or store the data. That is, this system depends more on the processing of the operating system. If the operating system becomes slow or corrupt for any reason, then we cannot access the data.

Indexed sequential file

As we have seen, sequential files have their advantages and direct files have their own. Both of these have some drawbacks and also some advantages. As the sequential file technique is easy to access, it does not have the overhead of address generation and its processing is not complicated. But at the same time, it is not suitable for large data sets. The direct file is more useful for large data sets even if there is overhead like address generation because where there is a large data set, there is a lot of time-saving in accessing the data.

Both file methods are used in indexed sequential order. In this, the operating system takes the help of an index. An index is a type of table, first of all, with the help of this table, the operating system searches the desired key field in a sequence, when the field is found, then its address is written next to it in that table. Now the operating system directly moves the head of the disk to the address location of the key field. In this way, we see that the sequence method is used while reading the index table and the direct method is used to access the address location.

This method is less complicated than direct file because it does not have to perform arithmetic operations related to address generation across the entire disk, but only till that location is reached.

Whatever the problem is, it is only in creating the index table, once the table is generated, then accessing the file becomes very easy.

We can understand this with an example of a very thick book that has thousands of pages.

If you have to read a particular chapter or topic of that book, then first of all you will take the help of the index given at the beginning of the book.

In that index, you will read the topic one by one using the sequence method.

When you will get your topic or chapter, then its page number will be written next to it, and then you will open that page number using the direct method.

In this system you use both sequence method and direct method when you search the topic in the index then you use sequence method when your topic is found related to that topic which page number is written till that page number you use the direct method to reach.

The same technique is also used in index sequential files So that we can take advantage of both the sequence and direct method.

At the same time, the disadvantages of both methods can be reduced to some extent.

This file organization method also works in conjunction with the operating system because index table generation and maintenance are possible only with the help of operating system programs.

This file organization technique is also known as Index Sequential Access Method (ISAM). For example, on a magnetic drum, the records on the track are stored sequentially. However, each record is assigned an index that can be used to access it directly.

Advantages of indexed sequential files

i. It combines the techniques of both sequential and direct files. It has the merits of both.

ii. It is a balanced technology, it has simplicity as well as fast access, and it is neither too complicated nor too simple.

iii. It is useful for both low data size and high data size

A disadvantage of indexed sequential files

i. As it is a combination of both sequence and direct techniques, the disadvantages of both are also included in this method.

ii. As a special storage device is required in the direct file method, in the same way, we also need a special type of storage device which supports direct storage and for this reason, it is also costly.

iii. Like a direct file, it also involves overheads such as address generation.

iv. It accesses the data at a slower speed as compared to the direct file.

9.3Master and Transaction file

Two types of files are used extensively in data processing or in a database management system, the master file, and the transaction file. As mentioned earlier, a database is a group of many related files although these are called normal files only. But if it is to be defined properly, then the database is mainly a group of many master files. The database is a collection of many related master files.

Because we generally use only the word file in the general sense, but in data processing, some special types of files are addressed by different names.

Two of the main ones are the master file and the transaction file.

Master file

Master file is the permanent file of a database. Which is the basis of many other types of files?

It is also called basic file because normally no change is done in the fields of these files.

With the passage of time, new requirements come and new files are created according to those needs.

But the one file that is initially created (master file) does not make any changes in it.

That is why the master file is also called a permanent file.

Transaction file

After the master file is created, the file related to other activities is called a transaction file.

These can also be called temporary files because they exist only until the master file is updated or the purpose for which an intermediate file is being created. Transaction files are created in large quantities in any database management system or data processing system, but their storage is not for a very long time.

These are stored only till their operation is completed. Some intermediate files are also required to be created while performing an operation; those intermediate files are called transaction files.

These are small files related to carrying out daily activities.

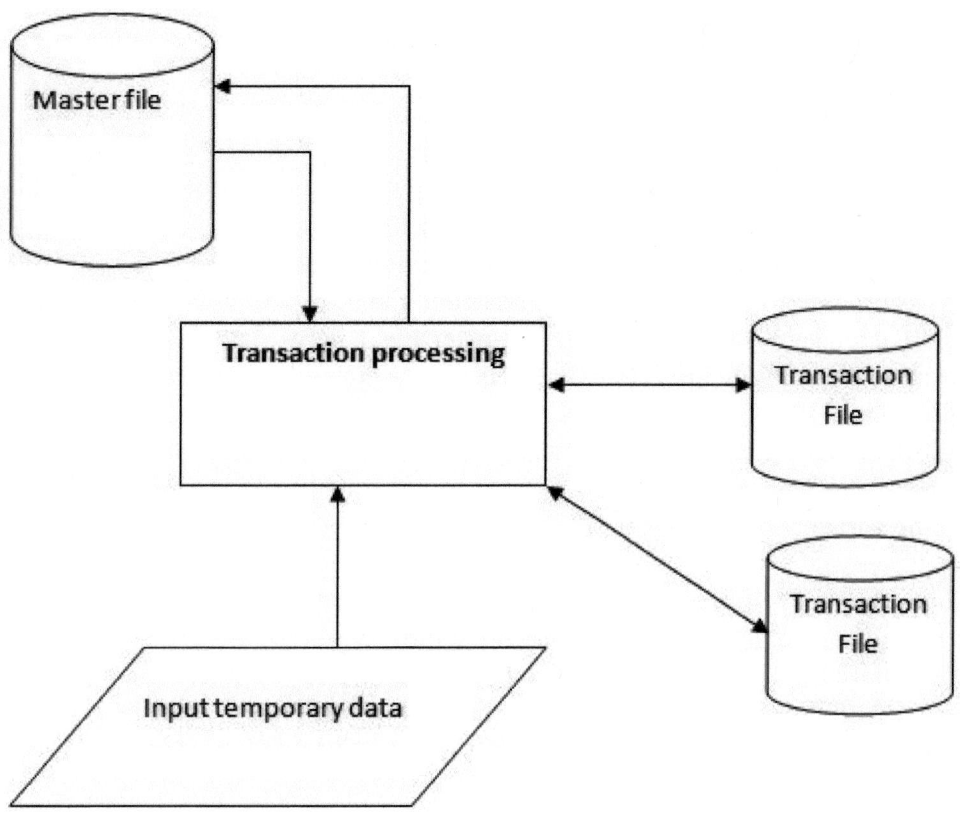

Transaction processing

For any transaction processing, system takes the required permanent data form master file, input some temporary data and create one or more transaction files for the purpose of performing transaction processing After updating the master file transaction process is completed.

Difference between master file and transaction file

> The master file is a permanent file of any database while transaction files are temporary files.

> The master file is created at the very beginning of any processing whereas the transaction file is created in the middle of the processing

> The master file is the basic file; it is the basis for all types of processing whereas the transaction file is created for the master file.

> The master file contains permanent information related to an individual whereas the transaction file contains temporary information.

> Master file has to be stored forever whereas transaction file is stored for a fixed time period only

> The master file remains useful even in absence of a transaction file whereas a transaction file cannot exist in absence of a master file.

We can also understand the difference between master file and transaction file with the help of the following example

For example, when a person goes to the bank to open his account, he is given a form.

That person fills the form and submits the form.

Now the bank employee creates a file of that person on the basis of the information filled in that form.

That file contains many types of information related to that person.

Such as his name, father's name, address, date of birth, permanent address, source of income, educational qualification, etc.

This is some basic information that is permanent, it does not change frequently.

Now on the basis of this information, a file of that person is created.

It is assumed that now that person has become the account holder of that bank, that person has been account holder on the basis of one file and the same file is called a master file.

Once the account is opened, the person now becomes the account holder of the bank.

Now it becomes the authority to do all the activities related to the bank.

That means depositing money, withdrawing money, transferring money to someone, etc.

In order to perform various activities in this manner, the bank employee also creates a file related to that person or related to the transaction.

But that file is called a transaction file and not a master file. Like that person sometimes comes to deposit some money, even for depositing money, the bank employee gives him a form, he fills the form, there is some information in the form also on the basis of that form the bank employee makes a file but it The file is only useful until the person's account is updated

That is, the amount of money he came to deposit is not credited to his account.

After that, after a few days, there is no justification for that file.

Similarly, if that person fills any form to transfer money to any person, the bank employee makes a file for that too; the justification of that file is only till that money reaches such a person.

After some time there is no justification for that file, then such a file (to deposit money, transfer money, etc.) will be called a transaction file.

In summary, we can understand that the file related to the personal information of an account holder in a bank is created at the time of opening the account in which his/her photograph, name, father's name, date of birth address, etc. is called a master file. Whereas the slip which is used while depositing or withdrawing money can be called a transaction file. Because that slip contains some temporary information like the date amount of the transaction etc. which is required only till the master file is updated after some time that slip is thrown away and they are of no use. Whereas the master file is kept safe as long as that person is the account holder of that bank.

Exercises

Objective type question

Choose the correct answer for the followings

1. Which of the following is the smallest data storage unit

(a) Field (b) record (c) character (d) file

2. Record is a set of many related________________ .

(a) Fields (b) records (c) characters (d) files

3. Database is a collection of ___________________.

(a) Field (b) record (c) character (d) file

4. Which of the following file organization method is the fastest method?

(a) Sequential (b) direct (c) indexed sequential (d) none of these

5. _______________ is an economical data storage device

(a) Tape drive (b) disk (c) drum (d) solid state drive

6. Permanent data is stored is this type of file

(a) Master (b) Transaction (c) Backup (d) Reference

7. Temporary data is stored is this type of file

(a) Master (b) Transaction (c) Backup (d) Reference

8. For direct access files which type of storage devises are to be used

(a) NTFS (b) FAT (c) ISAM (d) DASD

9. ____________ is suitable for large data set.

(a) Sequential (b) direct (c) indexed sequential (d) none of these

10. Any file organization method perform their operation with the help of ________

(a) DBMS (b) Operating system (c) data processor (d) file processor

Theoretical questions

1. What do you mean by data hierarchy? Explain with the help of an example.
2. Describe different data storage units with suitable examples.
3. List the advantages and disadvantages of the sequential file organization method.
4. Differentiate between direct and indexed sequential file organization methods.
5. Define mater and transaction files. With the help of suitable examples clarify the differences.
6. Explain different data storage devices in the light of sequential and direct file organization techniques.

CHAPTER TEN

WORD PROCESSOR

This chapter is dedicated to only word processors. In this chapter, we are going to know about various aspects of word processor software.

10.1 Introduction to word processor: First of all ,we have to know what exactly the meaning of word processor? The answer is based on two words i.e. word and processor.

Word: a meaningful collection of characters.

Processor: anything which can perform processing. Here the meaning of 'anything' means any software or hardware. But to better understand the meaning of processor we have to know the meaning of processing.

Processing - A series of actions or operations to complete a given task.

To understand the meaning of word processor, we need to understand the meaning of processing mainly because overall the word processing represents the whole computer system. Because the computer itself is called a data processor and we also know that the main device of our computer system is the processor itself. Just as a speaker is mainly used for voice, in the same way, a processor device is used for processing in a computer. Now just the question arises that what kind of processing work we get done from this device and the kind of processing work we get done with it, it becomes the same kind of processor. When the database is processed it becomes the data processor, when gets the audio data done it becomes the audio processor, if we get the processing of the image, then it becomes the image processor, if we get the processing of the video film, then it becomes video processor. All the programs associated with the computer system do some form of processing.

Processing is a systematic collection of many types of tasks. So word processing means software which is used to perform any type of useful operations on a word.' In another word, we can say that word-related operations can be performed using software that is called a word processor.

In solving math problems, in translating language, in solving a problem, in editing work, in making a broken machine, in doing any work, in doing work in a new way, In order to discover something new, to create or improve something new, etc., only one and only one thing is done --- that is processing.

Now let us talk about the application program in a computer system. Application programs are mainly made for the user of the computer. There are different types of computers and they have different types of requirements such as someone wants to make a drawing, someone wants to play a game, wants to record their voice. Someone wants to store his data; someone wants to use the Internet. In this way, we see that different types of application programs are made for different tasks in the computer system. Every application program has a major area of operation and their work areas are known as use application programs.

The software that controls the entire computer system is called an operating system. The software with the help of which we record the voice is called a sound recorder. The program through which you watch a movie or video file is called a media player. The application with which we paint is called a paintbrush. In the same way, a special program; a special processing program; that performs only and only word-related program is called a word processor.

We know that computer systems perform many types of processing tasks. Whether the processing of text, processing of voice, processing of photos, processing of video, or processing of database. The work of a computer system is to do processing and when we dedicate the task of processing to the word only and then this type of work is called a word processor.

10.2 Definition of word processor

A word processor is a dedicated software system for words only

A word processor is a kind of software that provides mainly input, editing, formatting, and output of text with some additional features.

A word processor is an application program that is used fundamentally for creating, editing, formatting and printing documents. Word processors have a lot of uses and applications in many business organizations, at home, and in educational contexts.

There are many types of application programs in a word processor, which are mainly related to a single word or many words. Like working or increasing the font size of a word, improving them, making them bold, underline them, or making them somewhat crooked (italic), etc. Thousands of functions are done with the help of any word processor software.

10.3 Features of a word processor

Word processor is software and many tasks can be done with its help, but there are some special functions that are necessary to be found in almost every word processor software because without them the word processor is considered incomplete. In other words, we can say that some essential features must be in any word processor. So here we will look at only those features which are required to be found in any word processor software.

To better understand the characteristics of a word processor, we can mainly divide it into two parts.

i. Basic features
ii. Advance features

> Basic features of word processor

- **CCP (cut copy paste)**

This is the biggest boon given by the computer to the world of official work, paperwork, or the world of writing. It is not an exaggeration to say that only because of this one feature, people left the use of a typewriter. Cut copy and paste is the most popular and very useful feature of the word processor. No word processor can be imagined without these features. So let's know what is cut copy and paste? And why is it so important after all?

The process of removing one or more words written in a document from one place is called cut.

To create a duplicate of one or more than one word of a document, the process of selecting those words is called copy. Its main purpose is to use the selected word again so that it does not have to be written again and again.

Reusing one or more words that have already been cut or copied is called paste.

If seen, the purpose of cutting or copying is to paste in the future.

We can understand cut copy paste with the help of an example, suppose two lists are being prepared, list one and list 2, 1000 names are written in the list. After some time the preparation of List 2 is done and it is found that there are 300 names of List 1 which are to be in List 2 also. So instead of rewriting the 300 names in List Two, those names from List 1 can be copied and pasted into List 2. Suppose that after some time it is known that some names were written in List 1 which should be in List 2, then those names of List 1 can be cut from there and pasted in List 2.

So in this way we see that cut copy paste is such a feature of word processors that saves us a lot of time and labor.

- **word formatting**

The process of writing the words written in a document in an attractive way is called formatting.

Formatting means; preparing the document according to a certain predetermined standard.

If said in easy language, writing the document in such a way that it is convenient for the reader to read the document.

While on one hand word processor helps us to prepare the document in an easy way, on the other hand, it also helps us in giving it an attractive look. Due to the convenience of formatting, we can also prepare many types of professional documents with the help of a word processor, such as writing a book, printing a card, preparing a pamphlet, etc., because, without formatting, our document does not look attractive.

The following are some of the most important tools for formatting that we find in any common word processor.

i. **Font face.**

Writing words in a particular way is called its font. Just as two people have different writings and by writing we know which person has written it, in the same way there is a system to support many types of fonts in word processors too. The user can select the font of his choice and prepare his document in the same way. In some places, if a particular type of font is required, then the user uses the same type of font for those places.

Example:

Word	font face
Hello	Calibri (Body)
Hello	**mangal**
Hello	Times new roman
Hello	Cambria (Headings)
Hello	Goudy Old Style
Hello	Eras Light ITC

Enter Caption

v. **Font size.**

Apart from selecting the desired font, we can also increase or decrease the size of the font as per our wish. Sometimes in a particular situation we need to write a particular word very big, then we can increase its size by selecting that word or sometimes there is a need that we have to write very small in a particular world, then we By selecting that particular world, you can reduce its size. As it is generally seen that the size of the heading is more than the normal words, then we select the heading and make its size more than the normal words so that it gets converted into a normal word heading.

Example:

Word	font size
Hello	5
Hello	10
Hello	14
Hello	28
Hello	72

Font color

Using different types of fonts, as well as changing their size, as well as changing their color in the word processor, allows because the main purpose of formatting is to make the document attractive. Colors have special importance for attractiveness; sometimes it becomes necessary to write them only with the help of bold italic underline or with the help of a special font, as well as to show them in a different color. Selecting the color of the font for those situations provides a special convenience. For example, the use of red color indicates a danger if some such words are used in the document and if they are displayed then they add beauty to the formatting of our document.

Example:

Word	font color
Hello	Black (default)
Hello	Red
Hello	Green
Hello	Blue

v. **Bold a particular text/word/sentence or whole document.**

To bold means to thicken a word. In between many words, sometimes we need to draw attention to a single word or text, and then in those situations, we bold the word so that that word attracts the attention of the reader. Bolding is an important part of formatting a word and any word processor provides us with this tool.

Example:

The examination will start at 10:00 AM sharp. In this sentence, 10:00 AM is written in bold because it needs more attention.

v. **Italicizing a particular text/word/sentence or whole document.**

Bold as well as writing a word in italics also attracts the attention of the user, it is seen that while writing the definition of a word in books, it is written in this manner. This is also an important part of formatting and the word processor provides us this facility.

Example :

The examination will start at ***10:00 AM*** sharp. Here 10:00 AM is written in BOLD as well as in italic style.

v. **Underline a particular text/word/sentence or the whole document.**

Underlining is a traditional way of formatting. Whenever a writer writes a document in a manual way and if he wants to attract the attention of the reader to any word or group of words in those documents, then he underlines those words or groups of words. That is, draws a long line under the sentence so that the attention of the reader goes specifically to those words, the same process can be done on the computer with the help of a word processor, it is called underlining.

Example:

The examination will start at ***10:00 AM*** sharp. Here 10:00 AM is written in BOLD and in italic style as well as also underlined to draw the attention of a reader.

v. **Alignment setting**

Writing words in a particular order is called alignment. For example, some people draw a line from the scale while writing so that whenever they reach a new line, it starts from a particular place. This makes the document nice to see. Alignment is mainly of three types Left Alignment Right Alignment and Center This means where do we start writing, although writing is mostly from left to right but on which side we want a straight line, this alignment shows Left Alignment In this, the entire document is in a straight line towards the left, in the same way in right alignment, the whole document looks like a straight line towards the right, in the same way in center alignment, the middle part is in a straight line. Its main purpose is to write the document in an attractive way, its main purpose is to make the document attractive. It gives comfort to the reader. If the alignment is taken care of, then our document will look very professional. it is also a very important feature of formatting.

Example:

Left alignment

Hello hello hello hello Hello hello hello hello Hello hello hello hello Hello hello hello hello Hello hello hello hello Hello hello hello hello Hello hello hello hello Hello hello hello hello Hello hello hello hellHello hello hello hello Hello hello hello hello Hello hello hello hello Hello hello hello hello Hello hello hello hello Hello hello hello hello Hello hello hello hello Hello hello hello hello Hello hello hello Hello hello hello hello

Right alignment

Hello hello hello hello Hello hello hello hello Hello hello hello hello Hello hello hello hello Hello hello llo hello Hello hello hello hello Hello hello hello hello Hello hello hello hello Hello hello hello hello Hello hello hello hello Hello hello hello hello Hello hello hello hello Hello hello hello hello Hello hello llo hello Hello hello hello hello Hello hello hello hello Hello hello hello hello Hello hello hello hello Hello hello hello hello

Center alignment

Hello hello hello hello Hello hello hello hello Hello hello hello hello Hello hello hello hello Hello hello hello hello Hello hello hello hello Hello hello hello hello Hello hello hello hello Hello hello hello hello Hello hello hello hello Hello hello hello hello Hello hello hello hello Hello hello hello hello Hello hello hello hello Hello hello hello hello Hello hello hello hello Hello hello hello hello Hello hello hello hello Hello hello hello hello

v. **Paragraph setting**

Paragraph settings play an important role in document formatting. We write a large document by dividing it into many different paragraphs. The use of paragraphs is a sign of good writing. We do the setting of where the paragraph starts, how much gap is between the paragraphs, how the paragraph ends, etc., with the help of paragraph setting. Using paragraphs makes our document very convenient to read, it is also an essential component of formatting.

v. Page setup

In a word processor, we prepare many types of documents because different types of documents are required at different places. Therefore, to write different types of documents, the setting of the page has to be done in different ways. For example, how much space is to be left on the left, right, top, the bottom side of the page (margin setting), what to write in the header and footer, etc The setting is done with the help of page setup. We can say that the process of setting up the page before creating the document is called page setup. With the help of page setup, we can determine in advance how much space we have to leave in the left and right of the document. There is no need to set up the page again and again.

v. Line spacing

While writing a paragraph, the amount of space to be given between two lines of a paragraph can be set with the help of this option. Once the line spacing setting is set, there is no need to do it again and again, it automatically leaves that much space between two lines. The writer can increase or decrease it according to his convenience.

v. Bullets

Many times while writing we need to list and numbering those lists and sometimes we prefer to use a special symbol instead of a number and bullet them. The facility of bullets is also provided in the word processor for formatting your document so that the list in the document can be made more attractive.

Example :

List of subjects

- Hindi
- English
- Commerce
- Money Banking
- Accounting

v. Border setting

Without borders, our document seems incomplete. We can say that the border setting provides a final touch to our formatting. Just like a book does not look good without binding, similarly, any document looks incomplete without a good border. This is also an important part of formatting.

Example:

Hello hello hello Hello hello hello.

- Find

Word processor software not only provides the facility of different tools to write the document, as well as provides many tools for us to read that document easily. One of those tools is the Find tool. Sometimes while reading a very large document, there is such a need that we have to search for a particular word, then instead of reading one line, with the help of a computer, that particular word can be reached in that document. This will save a lot of time.

Suppose ten lakh words are written in a document and suppose we have to find out only one name in them whether it is written in it or not? So imagine how difficult it would have been to find it humanely. The same computer will do this work in a fraction of a second. In fact, this is a unique example of the processing power of a computer.

- Find and replace

This option is used to make corrections in the document. This is a very useful tool provided by any word processor. With the help of this, we can not only search the desired word or words in the document but also replace them with a certain word or words. Many times it happens that while writing a document, a mistake is made again and again. In these circumstances, this option proves to be a boon because sometimes searching and changing different words becomes quite a complicated task. With the help of Find and Replace option, instead of searching those words separately, we write in one window which word to replace with which word. Word processor software does this task automatically.

Suppose we have a list of 1000 names in our document. Ajay's name should be removed and written Vijay due to mistake or any reason. And Ajay's name is written in 100 places. So imagine how difficult it would have been to find one name from a list of 1000 names and write another name in its place, but with the help of the word processor's fund and replace option, this task can be done in just a few seconds.

Find and replace tool is not only used to rectify the mistakes of the document but it can also be used to update the document. Because many times it happens that by making just a little change in the old document, it gets updated like if any data of the previous year is useful in the new year also, then we can change the name of that year from the previous year document to the new one. Enter the name of the year.

- **AutoCorrect**

This option automatically corrects common errors. This is yet another very useful feature provided by any word processor software. While writing a document, sometimes some common mistakes are made by the writer. Especially there are some words in English in which there is a possibility of most spelling mistakes, so instead of repeatedly checking them and giving suggestions to the writer, the word processor automatically corrects those mistakes and the writer does not even know. Let's go For example, if the computer is written while writing the spelling of the computer, then the word processor will automatically write it as its correct spelling computer.

The autocorrect option not only corrects the spelling but also keeps on making corrections while writing the document in many other places. For example, while writing a sentence, the first character should be in capital and if the writer writes it in small, then the word processor automatically converts it to capital letters. Similarly, if some grammar rules go wrong while writing the same, then the auto-correct option automatically corrects them.

- **Spelling check**

With the help of spell checking option, the writer can also write such English words whose spelling he does not know. Because as soon as we write the wrong spelling, the word processor shows us a red mark under that line, which is a symbol of wrong spelling? At the same time, it also provides the suggestion of spelling of the correct English word similar to the wrong spelling, with the help of which the writer of the document can choose the correct word, in this way we can say that with the help of word processor software writing a document becomes an easy task for any person.

- **Multimedia support**

The word processor is not only capable of processing words but also supports different types of media types. Because sometimes words do not work in a document, but to write an effective document, many types of shapes, diagrams, clip art, charts, images, pictures, and even videos are needed. Keeping these requirements in mind, the word processor provides us the facility to insert clip art, charts, images, pictures, and videos.

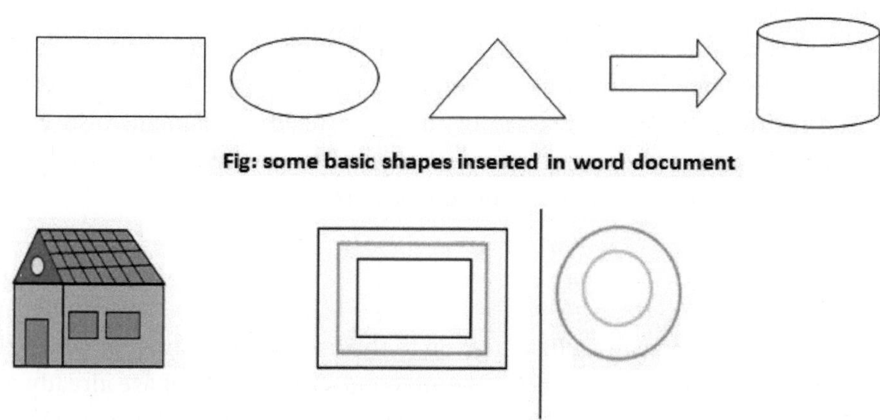

Fig: some basic shapes inserted in word document

Fig: some pictures inserted in word document

- Tables

Many times such a situation comes while writing a document when simple sentences are not effective for the presentation of information. Like displaying the timetable of a class or the mark sheet of a student, the table format is very useful in these situations. The table is a combination of row and column; through table we can present a lot of information very effectively by taking very little space. This is a traditional way of presenting the information. But even in word processors, it is available with different types of features. As we can insert columns and rows in any way we want. You can merge multiple columns or rows or split columns and rows. The Table feature is a very effective tool for any word processor.

A school Time table

A school Time table

Days/Periods	I	II	III	IV	V
Monday	Hindi	English	Mathematics	School Cinema	Computer
Tuesday	Science	English	Mathematics	School Cinema	Hindi
Wednesday	Hindi	English	Mathematics	G.K	Science
Thursday	Science	English	Mathematics	G.K	Computer
Friday	Hindi	English	Mathematics	G.K	Computer
Saturday	Science	English	Mathematics	G.K	Computer

Fig: use of table to show information

> Advance feature

By advanced feature, we mean their features of word processors which are not found in older versions of word processors. Or we can say that some new features have been added in the latest word processor software, we call those new features advanced features. With the passage of time, the needs of humans also increase, to meet the requirements; new features are also added to the software so that it can meet the needs of the user. Word processor software equipped with these new features is called advanced word processor software.

- **Import data**

In the new version of a word processor, such facility is given to the user with the help of which the data present in any other software can be imported. Many times such a situation comes that the database already exists and we want to use them again in a new document. So new documents, then again we can import all the databases directly instead of writing them in the word processor. Because many times it happens that our database is stored in a program and their number is very high and we have to use them in a word processor. In such a situation it was very difficult how to bring those data to the word processor. Therefore, in the new version of the word processor, an advanced feature was given, with the help of which the user could import the database.

- **Hyperlink**

As we know word processors are a very useful tool to create, edit and format a document. Instead of this, it is also very useful to read the documents.

With the help of hyperlinks, readers of the document can switch from one position to another position directly. Hyperlink provides the connectivity between two words or two-sentence or two pages or two documents or between a word page and web page.

A web page is a page of the internet that can be opened on a browser. Today's word processors also support Internet pages. That is why with the help of hyperlinks of word processors, we can connect web pages to software documents.

Generally, it is displayed in blue color which means if we click on a word that looks blue in color then the word processor will redirect us to somewhere else. By the way, it is mainly used to move from one place to another in the document. Used to navigate between places but mainly it is used to define the word. At the same time, it is also used as a table of contents on the main page in a very large document. Because it is seen many times in a book, a user does not read the entire book at once, but he has to read a particular topic. For this, he searches the topic written on the main page and if the topic is highlighted with a hyperlink, then by clicking on it, the reader directly reaches the page of the detail of that topic. This gives great convenience in reading .very large documents. From this, it can also be understood that while writing a large document, we should also keep in mind that we use hyperlinks.

- **Support many language**

Word processor software is mainly designed for the processing of words. But in the beginning, it mainly supported the English language only. This caused a lot of trouble to people working in other languages. Keeping these things in mind, many types of languages are supported in the new version of the word processor. Earlier this work was done only with the help of font but in today's word processor software, we can work in other languages also with the help of the latest technology.

Example :

A word 'computer' written in different languages.

Computer (English) कम्प्यूटर (Hindi) கணினி (Tamil) కంప్యూటర్ (Telugu) কম্পিউটার (Bengali) 電腦 (Chinese) Компьютер (Russian) L'ordinateur (Frence)

- **Voice typing**

Voice typing feature provides the facility to write by speaking instead of typing with the keyboard. As the name suggests, we type with the help of voice, that is, whatever we want to write, we just speak and the word processor will do it. Automatically types with the help of mice. Once the word is typed, it becomes like a normal word. After that we can do formatting etc. in it if we want. Although it does not have 100% accuracy yet, to a large extent it types with accuracy. In particular, it works quite accurately with online word processors.

Voice typing has completely changed the world of typing. Where on the one hand the computer in the beginning ended the typewriter machine because computers had innumerable advantages compared to typewriters. Similarly, now with the introduction of voice typing, the task of typing with the keyboard has reduced a lot. Because keyboard typing is considered to be a much older technique than voice typing. Keyboard typing also takes a lot of time. Voice typing not only saves time but also reduces the chances of mistakes and saves effort. Overall, voice typing saves a lot of money, time and labor. Voice typing is less to be praised. This modern word processor is a perfect example.

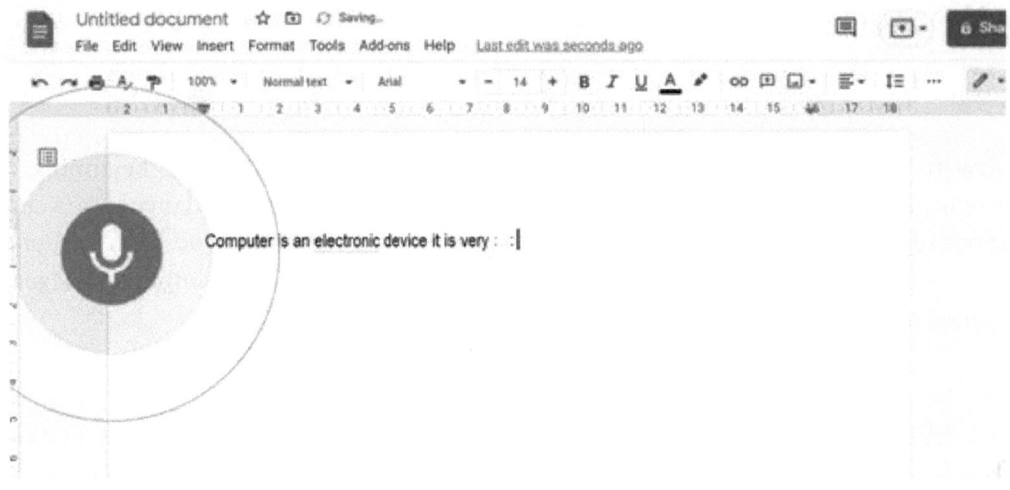

Fig: voice typing

- Macros

Macro is a very popular word processor tool which is used to record a series of commands.

While doing formatting type of work in the word processor, we have to give many commands one after the other. Like selecting the sentences and then increasing their size or font then, selecting the font, underlining bold italic, etc., etc. Sometimes the same type of work has to be done over and over again, which wastes a lot of time.

There is a facility to copy the content written in a basic word processor but the work done cannot be copied.

In the new version of the word processor, we can also copy the work to be done i.e. a set of commands, this is called macro.

With the help of this, we record the actions of the same type and whenever they have to be run, we run only a single macro command and the macro recorder automatically exits all the tasks. We can also call a macro "a collection of many commands". Many commands that we have to execute repeatedly in some sequence together, then in these circumstances we record all those work in one macro and whenever we need all those commands, we Execute the macro in which all the commands are recorded, so that all the work is done automatically. It is a very important tool of a word processor and it indirectly saves us a lot of time.

- Mail Merge

With this feature of the word processor, we can create personalized letters, envelopes for letters, wedding cards, and mailing labels of each person written on the mailing list. Sometimes we have to send the same letter with many different names and addresses. It means that 80-90 percent of the content of the document is common; there is only a slight difference between them. Like the name, address, etc. A wedding card is a good example of this. Everything is the same except the name of the one who is being given on the wedding card. So writing the same data, again and again, becomes a big problem.

Our solution to this problem lies in the mail merge feature. In mail merge, we write common content only once. And the data (such as the one to whom the card has to be given) is different, writes it in a separate database. And in the last merge them both. This saves time on the one hand, on the other hand also saves memory.

10.4 Difference between text editor and word processor

Although there is a lot of difference between a text editor and a word processor, still in some places it is considered the same, so it is very important to know what the basic difference between these two is.

Following are the important differences between a text editor and a word processor

i. Both text editor and word processor are application programs but text editor is inbuilt with the operating system whereas we have to install the word processor software separately.

ii. As the name of both shows, a text editor is used only for editing text. Editing means to make corrections i.e. in text editor we can do only minor corrective formatting Whereas a word processor is used to performing processing. Processing means; performing a series of actions to perform a certain task. Word processors have a lot of formatting features.

iii. A text editor is only in the form of a file. In this, all our work is done in just one file. In this, we cannot divide our work on the page. The length and width of its file are also not fixed. It will continue to write in a straight line until the Enter key is pressed.

In a word processor, we can work on many different pages. The file of a word processor is called a document. In this, the user can divide his document into many pages. Through page setup, we can already set the length, width, header, footer, margin, etc. We do not need to press enter key again and again.

iv. We call the content created in a text editor a 'file' whereas the content written in the word processor is called 'document'.

v. In text editor we cannot do formatting of any single character or text or word when word processor can do different formatting of each character of the whole document. That is to say, if 1000 lines are written in the text editor's file and we want to make a single line or single word or single character bold then it is not possible whereas in a word processor document, different formatting of one line, one word, and one character can be done.

Example

Computer

Fig: word computer is written using different formatting for each character. Not possible In text editor i.e. notepad.

i. Text editor supports only text format, in this, we cannot use any other type of data format like image, chart, audio, video file, clip art, diagram, etc. Whereas almost all types of data formats can be used in word processors. Word processors are made to support all types of data formats as well.

ii. Text editors are mostly used for system files whereas word processors are mostly used by external users.

iii. Text editor is a non-commercial application program whereas word processor is mostly used as commercial software. Word processors are mostly used in business applications.

iv. Text editor file extension is .txt while the extension of the word processor file is .doc

v. A very limited version of the text editor is available, while many versions of the word processor are available.

vi. The example of text editor is 'notepad' whereas 'MS-Word' is an example of a word processor.

vii. Notepad's file size is much smaller than the word processor's file size. So when we have to write only some normal text then instead of a word processor we think it is better to save the data in a text editor because it takes less memory.

10.5 Word processor example:

A word processor is a type of software. Software is called a word processor only when that software contains all the features of the word processor. But in reality, when a user wants to use a word processor, he will do an instance of it. As we know about the car. Do we know what a car is called? What are the features of a car? But when we go to buy it or want to use it, then just saying the car will not work. We have to tell the name of a car. Like Maruti, Indica, Alto, etc. . Similarly there are examples of word processor software. Just as a car is made by a different company, in the same way, word processor software is also developed by different companies or organizations. So let's know the examples of those different popular word processors.

Microsoft word:

Microsoft Word is the most popular name in the world of word processors. It is the most used word processor around the world; its popularity can be gauged from the fact that some people call it a word processor. It will not be an exaggeration if Microsoft Word is said to be synonymous with word processors because it is so widely used. The place that Microsoft Windows occupies in the world of operating systems is the same place Microsoft Word has in the world of word processors. MS-Word is very user-friendly word processor software. It is very easy to work on MS Word and it is also very easy to learn, hence it is called user-friendly. If you want to learn to work on a word processor, then it is very important that you have knowledge of Microsoft Word. However, nowadays many word processors have come into the market, most of which are also available online. But the place of Microsoft Word is still visible in the sky of the word processor like a shining star.

Microsoft WordPad

Microsoft WordPad is also word processor software developed by Microsoft Corporation. But Word document has very few features as compared to MS Word, although a lot more features are available than Notepad, we can say that it is a lite version of MS Word.

Microsoft Works

Microsoft Works is also a word processing software program developed by Microsoft itself. Microsoft Works began to be used as an alternative solution to Microsoft Word due to the cost difference between the two different software. Both Microsoft Works and Microsoft Word use different file formats. The default Microsoft Word document format is DOC or DOCX, while Microsoft Works uses the WPS format. Although not in use nowadays. Microsoft discontinued the development and distribution of Microsoft Works in 2007.

Apple TextEdit

TextEdit is a text editor and word processor software. It comes with Apple MacOS X computer that allows you to create, view, edit, and modify text files and documents. The editor allows you to format text, create tables, import graphics, work with HTML, and even add multimedia files like music and movie files.

AppleiWork

iwork is an office suite used in Apple computers and Apple iPhones. There are many different types of software used in this, such as numbers for keynote presentations, for spreadsheet programs, in the same way, it has a separate program for pages which is used for a word processors. It is mainly available in builds with the Apple iPhone operating system and does not support Microsoft.

Google Docs

A Google doc is the most advanced word processor of the modern era which was developed by Google Corporation. It is online free word processor software. Online means it is web-based application software and need not install onto your computer. Anyone who wants to use Google Docs word processor can use it directly with the help of an internet connection. But we need the internet to use Google Docs. Being a web-based application; it can be accessed only through the internet.

It has almost all the features of traditional word processor software and along with them; some advanced features are also available which are not found in traditional word processors. Its program quality is also far more advanced than traditional word processors.

There are mainly three features found in Google Docs, first, it can be used online. Second, it is available for free, for this you do not need to spend any money, you just need to have an internet connection and thirdly it provides a cloud storage facility. In cloud storage, the user can store his data and access it from anywhere as it was not in the traditional storage system because in cloud storage our data is from the Internet and not in the hard disk of the system.

Due to being stored in the cloud, we can access our data from anywhere. With this, there is no problem with carrying data. Apart from the above three main features, there are some other features which are as follows.

> It supports multiple document formats. That is, regardless of the application in which the document file is created, it gets opened in Google Docs with some modifications. Google automatically makes that file format supportable so that the user can get the facility to read the content.

> Google Docs supports .doc, .docx, .docm .dot, .dotx, .dotm, .html, .txt, .rtf, and .odt files.

>We can also share the document of Google Docs among many remote users.

> Multiple users can access a document in Google Docs, so it is also a multi-user document. That is, more than one user can contribute to the preparation of a single document.

OpenOffice**(writer)**

WPS office

WPS Office is an office suite application software supporting Microsoft Windows, macOS, Linux, iOS, and Android, developed by Zhuhai-based Chinese software developer Kingsoft.WPS Office is made up of three primary components: WPS Writer, WPS Presentation, and WPS Spreadsheet.wps writer is used for word processing. Although it supports many operating systems, it is very popular mainly in Android mobile phones. In the world of mobile phones, it is similar to MS-word. It supports many types of document formats like WPS, WPT, doc, dot, Docx, dotx, docm, dotm.

10.6 Word processor applications

Although there are countless applications of word processors, some of the most useful applications are as follows.

Desk top publishing (DTP)

DTP is mainly used in the publishing industry. Before the advent of computers, the work of printing in the publishing industry was done manually, this was a much more difficult task than today. Preparing the document, improving it, and printing it in the last, all these three tasks were done with the help of many types of mechanical devices without a computer. But after the invention of the computer, the nature of the publishing industry has completely changed. We can say that after the advent of the computer, the publishing industries benefited the most because it is used from writing documents to improving them to printing. After the advent of computers, computers changed the world of the publishing industry. The software with which the publication work is done on the computer is what we call DTP software. Although many types of software come into use in DTP, we cannot say that single software can perform all the functions of DTP, but the place of a word processor is highest in the desktop publishing industry.

DTP is a kind of software system used for creating, editing, compiling, and formatting documents using the page layouts method on a desktop computer.

It was initially used in print publications, that is why it came to be called Desktop Publishing and its name of this type of software became DTP Software that creates or edits documents, improves them or prepares their page setup or all such software used in printing comes under DTP. DTP is a group of different types of software. Initially, the software which was used in the printing of publications was called DTP software, but nowadays they are also used in the preparation of online content. We can say that It is a digital version of the traditional printing industry.DTP allows individuals, business groups, financial institutions, and other many organizations to self-publish a wide variety of impressive content.

With the help of DTP, the quality of normal text and images can be improved, the same content will be there, but if it is prepared with the help of DTP, then its quality will be much higher, we can say that quality content is prepared with the help of DTP. As mentioned earlier, DTP is not called anyone software, it is a group of software, and a word processor is also one of that software. The DTP method provides more control and command over design, layouts settings, and implementation, and typography than individual word processor software. But the share of word processor software in DTP is higher than any other software.

Adobe PageMaker, Adobe InDesign, Adobe FrameMaker, and Corel Ventura are some popular names of DTP software. Although the word processor cannot be called DTP software completely, the main contribution of the word processor in the work of DTP is because there are many similarities between the functions of DTP and the functions of the word processor. A large part can be done by word processors because the tasks that are done both in DTP and in Word are related to preparing documents, improving them, formatting them and we know that the world in word processors. Key processing provides related tools; they are also used in DTP.

Book publications, visiting cards, marriage cards, pamphlet designs, etc. are some examples of DTPs, as well as those prepared with the help of word processors. Direct indirect all the work related to Document comes in the category of DTP and they can also be prepared by a word processor, so we can say that word processor application is the most used in the field DTP.

Individual.

In general, word processor software is mostly used by individuals. The main reason for this is that there are some readymade templates available in different types related to different areas. This makes it much easier for an individual to act on a personal level. With the help of a ready-made template, any person can prepare many types of documents in a standard way without the help of any other person. Such as business cards, applications for many types, legal notices, resumes, official letters, etc. Because of this, word processor software proves to be very useful for ordinary people, so it is used a lot at the individual level.

Book writing

There are many such features in word processor software that are designed to keep book writing in mind. The main among them is Grammar and Spelling Checking. Because when a writer writes a book, instead of spelling and grammar, he pays attention to the writing flow, his order of thought should not be broken because if he keeps in mind the translation and spelling, then the chain of his thoughts breaks, so the chain of thoughts should be maintained. To keep the word processor software either automatically corrects the spellings or indicates it with a red mark so that later the writer can get it corrected by himself or by someone else. Word processor is also used a lot in the world of book writing or by writers, it is considered to be very popular software in the world of writers. Word processor is wonderful software in the field of writing and it is used in abundance. It is a wonderful application in the field of book writing.

Office work

In-office work, suppose the word processor is an essential part. In today date, no office can run without word processor software because all the work of the office depends on the document, and documentation-related work is done by word processor software. Therefore, the word processors can never be ignored in office work because, on the one hand, this word processor software gives many types of templates in thousands of ways, due to which the time of the employees is saved and in any organization in which this work is done. It's being done saves time and for any office, there is nothing more precious than time for any organization and to save time, many tools have been given in it, the most important of them is copy-paste. It is like a lifeline for office work. It is used as a heartbeat. It saves more time than imagined and another main reason is the role of the word processor in-office tasks that is the storage solution it provides.

Academics

Word processor software is also used indiscriminately in the academic field. Such as preparing question papers, preparing mark sheets,s and preparing documents related to various types of academic and examinations. The use of word processors is very common, in today's date, there are different types of universities, colleges, coaching institutes, primary level schools, any institution related to academics, where the help of word processors is taken.

Knowing so many features, no need to tell how it helps them. It can be easily understood that why the word processor is so helpful in preparing the documents of the Academy. The biggest reason for the use of word processors in academics is security because confidentiality occupies a prominent place in universities, colleges, etc. and word processor software also provides the features of security because the content of the question paper can be written anywhere but it should be kept confidential. Keeping it properly, sending it from one place to another, etc. is the most security concern and word processor software has been designed keeping in mind the security. The document that will be created in any word processor software can be protected with the help of a password.

Research paper

Word processors are used extensively in academic as well as research areas because research papers are mostly presented at the national and international levels and standardization has a prominent place there because if those papers are not written in the standard way then they cannot be published in an International journal etc. It is used by researchers all over the world because it contains all the tools useful for preparing standard documents, such as different types of fonts, font size alignment, paragraph setting, etc. Standard formatting is very important for writing a research paper and word processing software provides us all the necessary tools to do standard formatting, so it proves to be a powerful weapon for writing a research paper.

Exercises

Objective type question

Choose the correct answer for the followings

1. MS-word is a ___________.

(a) Driver software (b) operating system (c) Spreadsheet (c) Word processor

2. Notepad is known as

(a) Text editor (b) word processor (c) writing tool (c) driver software

3. Which of the following is not an important function of word processor?

(a) Sound editing (b) text alignment (c) auto correct (d) spelling checking

4. The size of a word is referred as a _____________ in word processor.

(a) Font face (b) font size (c) font color (c) text size

5. Which of the following is used for List formatting in word processor?

(a) List style (b) list type (c) list trigger (c) Bullet

6. ___________ enables users to directly move from one location to another location.

(a) hyperlink (b) find and replace (c) goto (e) None of these

7. An important features of word processor which is used to record a series of commands.

(a) Command recorder (b) record data (c) macro (e) none of these

8. Google Docs is an example of

(a) Web browser (b) word processor (c) search engine (d) text editor

9. WPS office is a ______________

(a) Office suite (b) word processor (c) text editor (d) all of these

10. MS-word is developed by _______________

(a) Open source community (b) Google corporation (c) Microsoft corporation (d) none of these

Theoretical questions

1. What do mean by word processor? List the name of some popular word processor software.

2. Explain some important applications of a word processor.

3. Differentiate between a text editor and a word processor.

4. What are the functions of word processor software?

5. What is mail merge? Explain with example.

6. Write a short note on document formatting.

7. Describe the term DTP and explain how to word processor software is useful for it.

CHAPTER ELEVEN

DATA COMMUNICATION AND NETWORKING

Each person has his own separate existence his appearance, color, length, age, weight, knowledge, etc. But there is one quality of man which alone is of no use and that is communication. At the same time, it is also an essential quality. At least two persons are required for communication. Just as communication is important in normal life, in the same way, communication has very special importance in the computer world. Just as we convey our words to others through dialogue, at the same time the words of others also reach us. In the same way, in the computer world also a computer establishes communication. Just as human life would have been deserted without communication, in the same way, the computer world would also be deserted without communication. In this chapter, we will learn about computer interaction.

12.1 Introductions to data communication and networking

Data communication is the exchange of data between two devices through a transmission medium.

In networking, the physical connection between computing devices is established through cable media or wireless media.

Data communication is the process of transporting data from one node to another.

A network is a communication system designed to send data from an origin point to a destination point.

The best example of a computer network is the Internet. Computers are used to generate information. The information it generates is not useful in itself. This information should be given to the right person at the right time. Information often needs to be transmitted from one place to another. This process is called Data Communication. It makes our daily life very easy.

Characteristics of Data Communication:

The effectiveness of a data communication system depends on three characteristics:

i) Delivery:

The system should distribute the data to the correct destination. This data should be accessible to the intended device or user only.

ii) Timeliness:

The system should deliver the data on time. Late-delivered data is useless in the case of video, audio, and voice data, being delivered on time means delivering the data in the same order as the data is produced, and without delay.

iii) Accuracy:

The system must send the data correctly. If the data is changed in transmission then it is unusable. Data should arrive at the destination as it is sent. If the data is changed in the middle it is more harmful than not reaching it.

Components of Data Communication

Communication is a system. And it requires different components to run smoothly. Its five main components are as follows.

i) Transmitter:

The transmitter device sends the message. It can be a computer, mobile phone, workstation, telephone, video camera and anything else. Sometimes it is referred to as a node.

ii) Receiver:

The receiver receives the message sent by the transmitter. It can also be a computer, mobile phone workstation, telephone handset, television, and anything else.

iii) Message:

A message is a transmission (data) that is to be communicated. It can contain text, numbers, images, sound, or video, or whatever.

iv) Medium:

The transmission medium is the physical path through which a message travels from sender to receiver.

It can be twisted-pair wire, coaxial cable, fiber optic cable, laser, or radio wave (terrestrial or satellite microwave).

v) Protocol:

The protocol is a set of rules for data communication. It is representative of an agreement between communication devices. Without the protocol, two devices can be connected, but cannot communicate, just as a person who understands Hindi will not communicate with a person who doesn't understand the Hindi language. A common language and rule must be known by both of the participating persons of communication.

12.2 Transmission media

Transmission media is a path of transmission of information from the sender to the receiver. It is of two types:-

A:-wired

B:-wireless

A:-wired:-

The transmission media in which the connection between two devices is done by a physical methods such as cable or wire is called wired transmission media. It is also called guided media.

These are of the following types:-

(a):- coaxial cable

(b):- fiber-optic cable

(c):- twisted pair

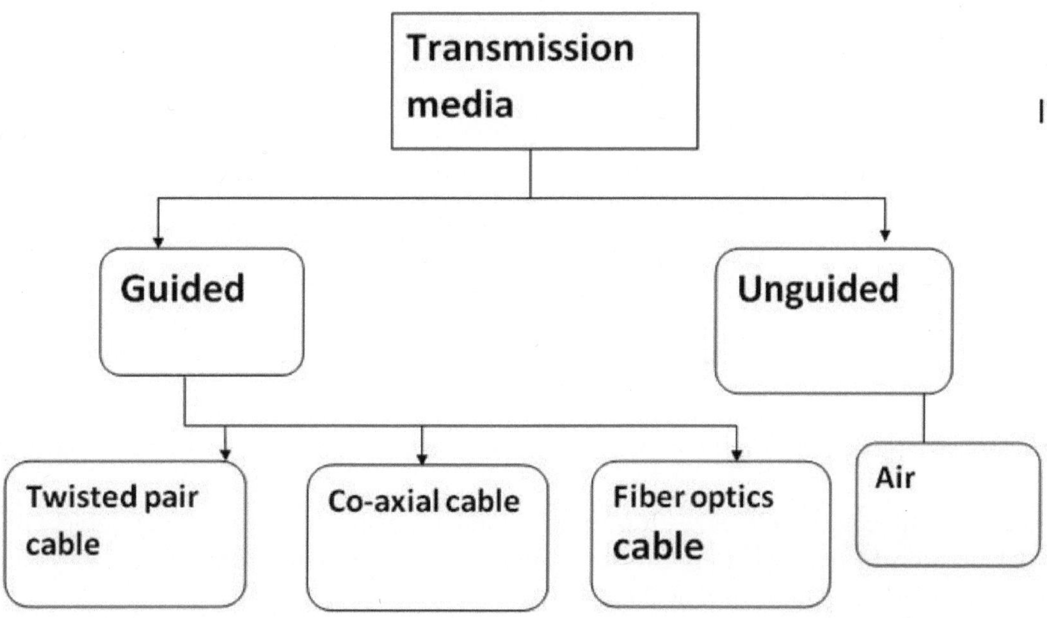

Enter Caption

(a):- Twisted pair:-

It is a copper wire or cable in which two insulating wires are made by wrapping them between each other. Due to the wrapping, there is no interruption in the signals of both wires. This cable is used in old telephone lines.

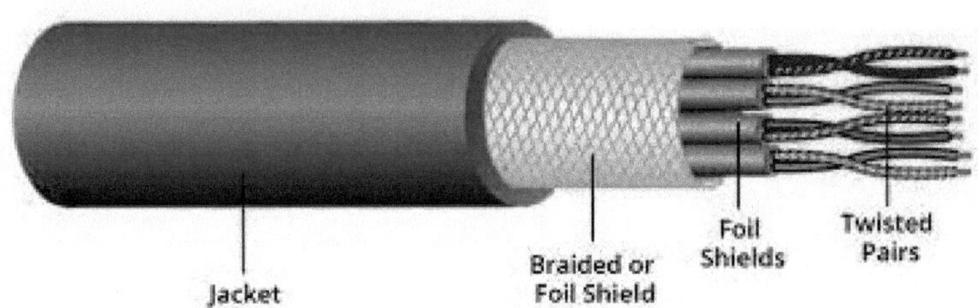

(b):- coaxial cable:-

It consists of a hollow tube of a conductor. And the second conductor is installed inside the hollow tube coaxially on its axis. The dielectric between these stars is solid or gaseous. In coaxial cable, the inner conductor is surrounded by the outer cylindrical hollow conductor. The main advantage of a coaxial is that the magnetic and electric fields remain inside the external conductor and do not leak into the free space, due to which the radiation is completely eliminated. Apart from this, the external conductor also generates effective electromagnetic shielding from the external electric magnetic signal.

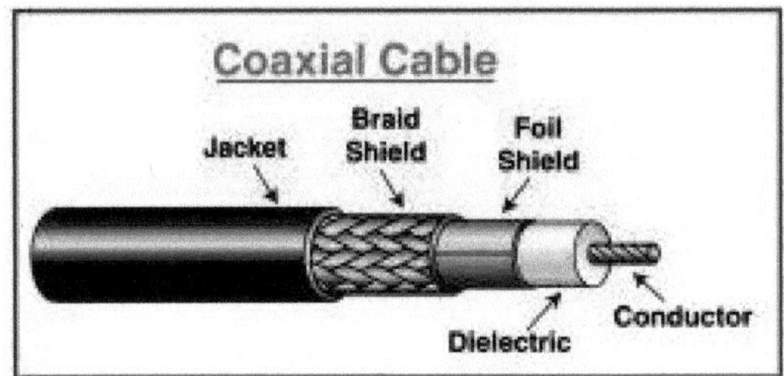

The dielectric loss also Increases with the signal frequency. This is very frequently used in cable TV set up.

(c):- fiber-optic cable:-

This cable is based on fiberglass technology. It is very fast and it is also known as nest gen cable. Fiber-optic cable is made of glass or plastic which is called optical fiber. These cables carry data from one place to another through light signals. These cables are designed for long distances.

When a beam of light enters in a certain direction from one end of a transparent rod, the beam of light undergoes total internal reflection several times on the surfaces of the rod and the beam of light remains inside the rod. In this way, when the beam of light reflected many times comes out from the other end of the rod, there is no loss of intensity of light. This type of rod is called fiber.

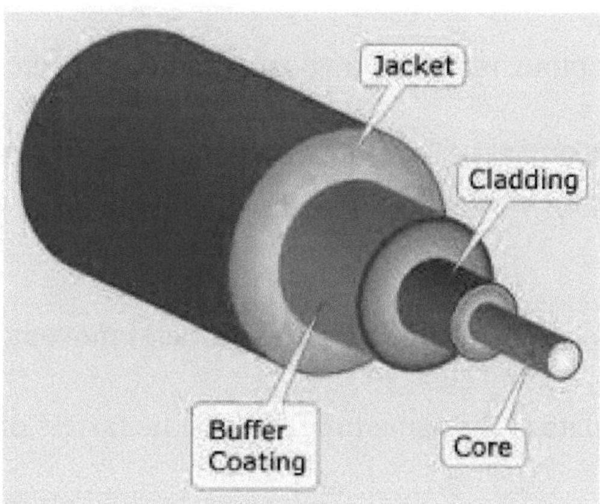

B:-wireless:-

That transmission media in which no physical contact is required, that is, in which communication takes place without wires is called wireless transmission media. It is also called unguided media. Mainly it uses air to send data. A mobile phone is the best example that uses wireless media to send or receive voice signals or digital data. Bluetooth technology is also based on wireless media.

These are of the following types:-

(a):-Radio waves

(b):-microwaves

(c):- infrared waves

(a):-Radio waves:-

They are easy to install and have high attenuation. Radio waves are mostly Omni directional. When an antenna transmits radio waves, they propagate in all directions.

Radio waves are used in the communication of television, mobile, and radio. They have a radio tuner that receives radio waves and converts these waves into mechanical vibrations in the speaker, due to which we hear sound from the speaker.

(b):-Microwaves:-

In this, information is transmitted by electromagnetic waves whose wavelength is measured in centimeters.

Their frequency exceeds 1GHz and they are made up of many types of transmit. Microwaves are used in cooking and mobile etc. and it is also used in wifi.

(c):- Infrared waves:-

It is electromagnetic radiation of a particular wavelength which we call infrared. Humans cannot see these waves but can feel them in the form of heat in the skin.

They are used in TV remote control, wireless LAN, CCTV, and missile guidance systems, etc.

12.3 Transmission mode:-

The direction in which data or information is transmitted from one place to another is called transmission mode. It indicates the direction of the flow of information. It is also called communication mode.

Simplex

It is of three types:-

simplex:-

Half-duplex

Full duplex

Simplex

Simplex means that communication will be in one direction only. That is, the sender can only send the data but cannot receive it.

Example: - Radio, TV transmission, remote, monitor, keyboard, and mouse, etc.

II:-half-duplex:-

In half-duplex, we can send and receive data in both directions but only in one direction at a time. That is, both send and receive cannot be done at the same time. This mode is sometimes also called semi-duplex.

Half Duplex

or

Example:-walkie-talkie only one person can talk at a particular time of movement.

III:-full duplex:-

In this, we can also send and receive data at the same time. This is the fastest directional mode.

Full Duplex

Example:-Telephone communication system or mobile phone is an example of this where two persons can talk to each other at the same time.

12.4 Networking devices

Networking devices are devices by which two or more computers or electronic devices are connected so that they can communicate with each other by sharing data.

Following are some important networking devices.

Repeater

Hub

Bridge

Switch

Router

Repeater

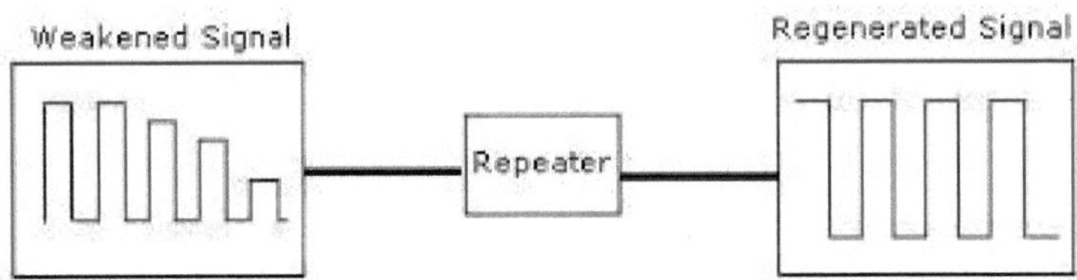

Enter Caption

A repeater is a networking device that receives a data signal and replays and forwards that signal. The repeater is used to revive the signals to a certain extent before they are lost. The signal is regenerated because when the signal is weakened from place to place, it is therefore resold before the signal is weakened or destroyed so that the signal is not destroyed. It supports both digital and analog signals. It can repeat and revive the signals. In other words we can say that it powers the incoming weak signals.

There are two types of repeater analog repeater and digital repeater.

The analog repeater can only amplify the weak signal. Whereas the digital repeater reconstructs the signal and sends it forward by removing errors from it.

Hub

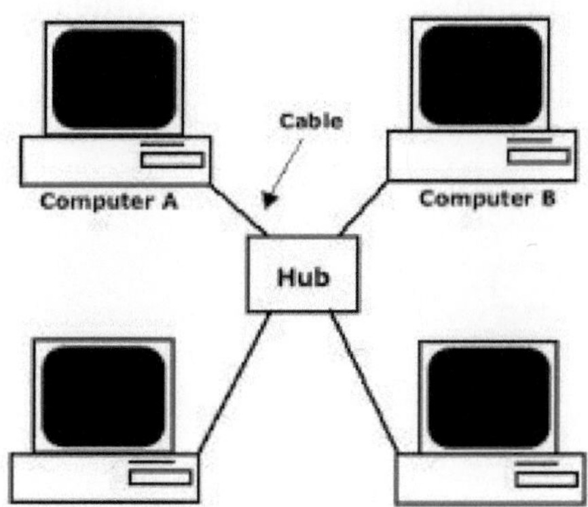

Enter Caption

Hub is also a networking device that is used to connect many computers or networking devices together through cable.

There are many ports in the hub. The hub sends the incoming data packets from any one port to all the other ports. It is up to the receiving computer (port) to decide whether the packet is intended for it or not.

If we have to send data from computer 1 to computer 2 then as soon as computer 1 sends data then the hub does not check that what is its destination it sends these data signals to all other computers (2,3,4,5...) sends. Computer 2 takes these data signals while other computers ignore them.

Hubs are used to connect different computers in a local area network (LAN) in a star or hierarchical topology or mesh topology.

Bridge

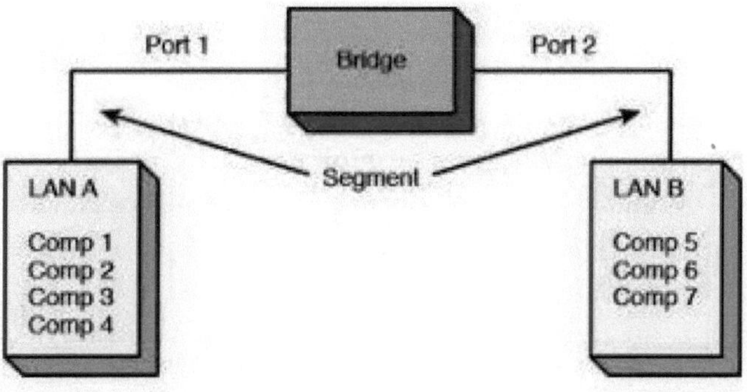

It is a networking device that connects network segments together. And also does the work of data filtering.

The bridge has only two ports, an incoming (incoming) and outgoing (outgoing).

The bridge checks the destination address before sending the data. If the bridge gets the destination address then it sends the data otherwise it will not transmit the data.

Bridges are used to extend the network while maintaining data signals and traffic.

Switch

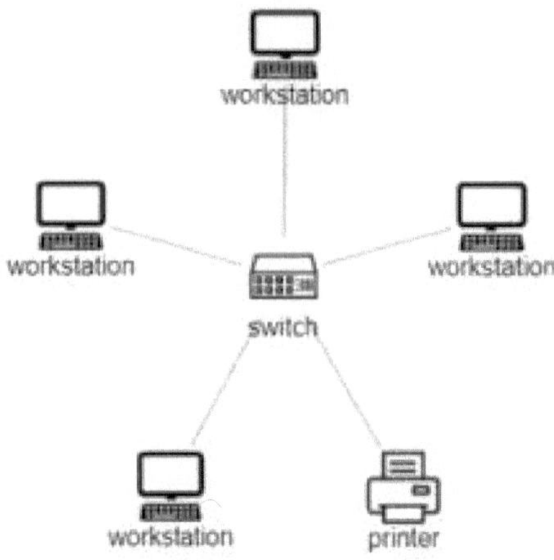

A switch is a networking device that connects networking devices and computers. It is very much similar to bridge and hub. It is also called a multiport bridge because its mechanism is similar to that of a bridge and hub.

There are many ports in the switch, when the data comes through the switch, the switch reads the address of the destination computer in the data and sends it to the destination computer

Switches reduce traffic. And the collision divides the domain into segments.

Switches have built-in hardware chips that perform the function of switching. Its speed is very fast and they come with many ports.

In this, the data goes in the form of frames and it also does data filtering like a bridge.

Router

A router is a networking device used to provide the routes of incoming data packets.

A router is an internetworking device that connects two or more networks.

A router is a device that provides routing of data. The data of the Internet or network goes from one place to another through this. A router has an inbuilt program with the help of which data is sent from one network to another. This networking device can work on different protocols.

If the destination of the data packet is on another network then the data packet will be sent from the router, so the internet does not work without the router. It is like a traffic controller of data packets of the whole computer network.

The main function of the router is to find the shortest distance to reach the data to its destination. The router does this work with the help of a table. The table contains the distances between all the connecting nodes. The router determines the distance due to this table and sets the path between the sources of destination. There are mainly two types of router static router and dynamic router.

Static router:

Static routers are called those who maintain their tables only once after being on. After that, there is no change in their tables as long as they remain on.

Dynamic router

Dynamic routers maintain the table after it is turned on but at the same time keep updating the table periodically. A dynamic router proves to be more effective than a static doctor as it decides the route according to the current state of the network.

12.5 Network topology

Network topology means the shape of the network. This means how the nodes (computers) or devices used in the network will connect to each other and transfer data among themselves, it is called network topology.

TYPES OF TOPOLOGY

There are six types of Network Topology-

i. **Bus Topology**
ii. **Star Topology**
iii. **Ring Topology**
iv. **Mesh Topology**
v. **Tree Topology**
vi. **Hybrid Topology**

Bus Topology

In this topology, there is a centralized cable and in that centralized cable, all the computers are connected. This topology is visible from the outside like a straight line in form of the bus; hence it is called bus topology. In that centralized cable, all the computers are connected through T-Connector. Used in EX- Broadband communication, cable connection.

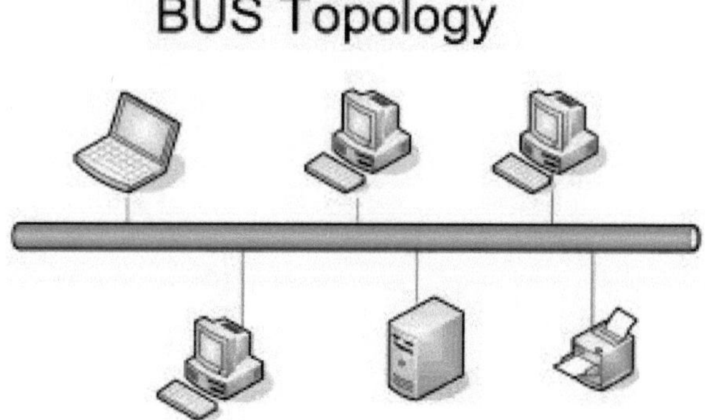

Enter Caption

Advantage of Bus Topology

• It is very simple to implement.

• This topology is easy to implement or installation and you will get all the components used in it easily.

• If a problem occurs in one computer, then the rest of the computer used in the network will not have any effect.

• You will not need any dedicated device (meaning switch, hub) to implement this. In this topology, all the computers are connected with the cable only.

• If there is any problem in this topology, it is easy to solve that problem.

Disadvantage of Bus Topology

• Everything is based on a single cable wire.

• The biggest disadvantage of this topology is that if something happens to the centralized cable or if this cable is cut, then the whole network will be shut down.

• In this topology, if you are sending anything to any dedicated computer, that thing will be sent to all the computers connected to the network.

• The higher the number of computers in this topology, the slower the data communication of this topology will be.

• In this topology, if anyone wants to add or remove a computer, then the whole network will go down.

Star Topology

Star topology is a very popular topology in LAN networks. This topology is most used in today's time. What happens in this is that all the computers are connected through a centralized device (a centralized device can be any switch or hub). That centralized device connects all the computers and communicates among them.

The advantage of this topology is more and the disadvantage is less, so this topology is used the most of the area like school lab, office, bank or railways computer network.

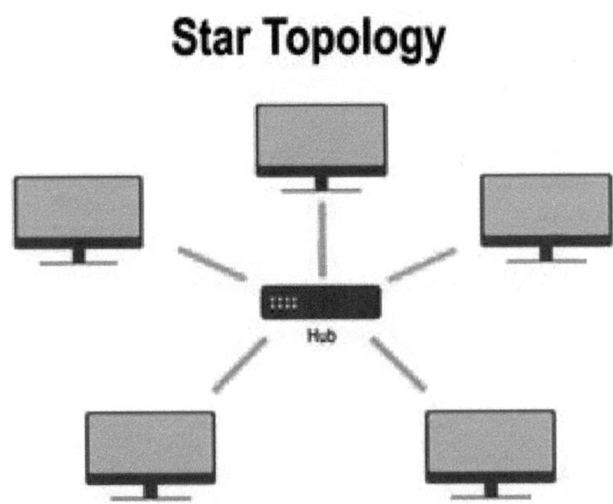

Advantage of Star Topology

• It is very reliable. Like bus in this everything is not depend on one wire cable.

• The requirement for cable is very less.

• With the help of this topology, you can also create huge networks.

• This is not a complicated topology; you will understand everything very easily.

• If there is any problem in the network, you can solve it easily.

• Its biggest advantage, if you want to add a computer or remove a computer, then there will be no difference in the network. This means an extension of the network is very easy.

Disadvantage of Star Topology

1. Its only disadvantage is if the centralized device is bad, then the whole network will be suffered.
2. Installation cost is high.
3. A separate device is needed for network setup

Ring Topology

This is a circle shape-based topology. That's why it is called ring topology. Ring topology is similar to bus topology but in a ring topology, the last computer connects with the first computer. In-ring topology, each device is connected to other devices by forming a circular structure. The way of transferring data in this topology is that a computer receives data from the previous computer and sends it to the next computer.

In this topology, all the computers transfer clockwise data to other devices. Each computer or node of the network acts as a repeater to transfer data

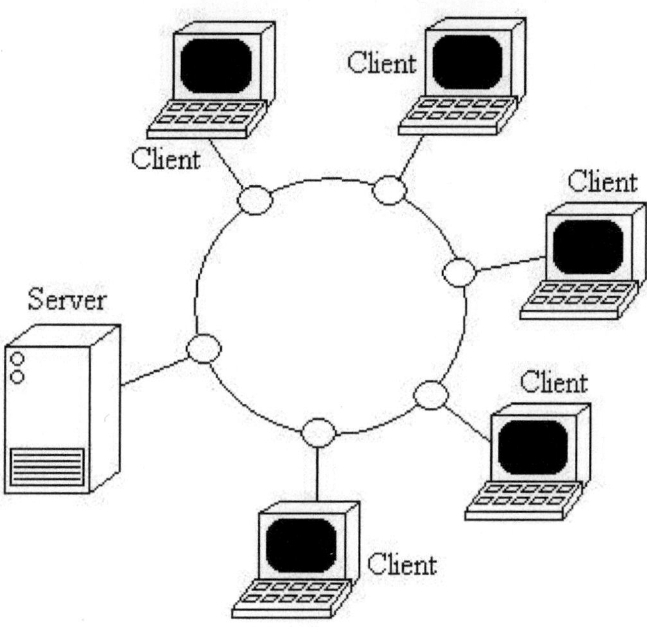

Advantage of Ring Topology

1. Its installation cost is less.
2. You do not need any dedicated device (meaning switch, hub) to implement this. In this topology, all the computers are connected through the backbone cable itself.
3. If there is any problem in this topology, it is very easy to solve that problem.

Disadvantage of Ring Topology

1. The biggest disadvantage of this topology is that if something happens to the centralized cable or if this cable is cut, then the whole network will be shut down. Same as bus topology.
2. In this type of topology, if you want to add or remove a computer, then the whole network will goes down.
3. The higher the quantity of computer in this topology, the slower the data communication of this topology will be.

Token Ring Topology

It is based on a token system. It is used more than ring topology. In this, all the computers are connected through a centralized device that centralized device works to give tokens to all the computers. The computer with the token will be able to talk to any computer connected to the computer network. Any device that does not have the token will not be able to talk with the computer. That centralized device works to give tokens.

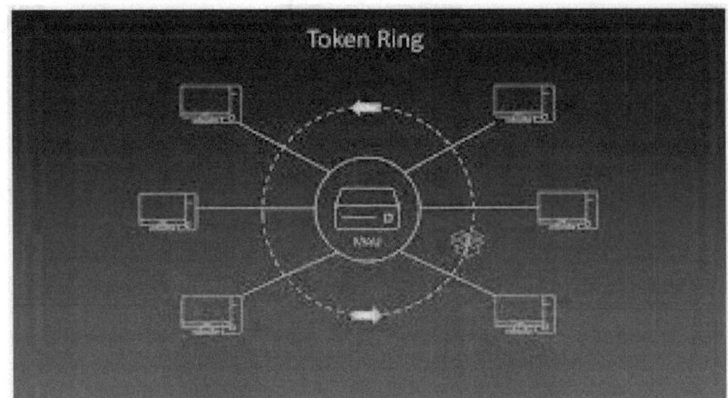

Mesh Topology

It is a mixer topology. In Mesh topology, you have to remember only one thing that every computer used in it is connected with another computer through a dedicated line. In the previous topology, we saw that if a device wants to talk to another device, then with the help of another device, we knew by talking. But in this, the help of no device is taken; they use the dedicated lines of that computer to talk. EX- This topology is used for Router connection.

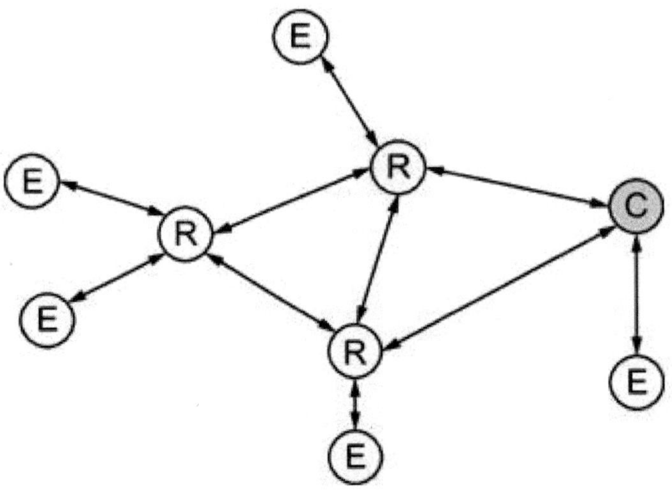

Enter Caption

Advantage of Mesh Topology

1. This topology is very reliable because there are so many routes that can reach a single node.
2. The data communication speed of this topology is fast as compared to the rest of the topology.
3. There is no disruption in the network at the time of adding a new device or removing a device.
4. This topology is very secure.
5. Only if anyone breaks down, then the rest of the computer or network is not affected at all.

Disadvantage of Mesh Topology

- This topology is very robust, it is not easily understood.
- This topology is very complicated.
- Wiring is very complicated
- The cabling cost of this topology is high.
- If there is a problem with this topology, it is difficult to find out that problem.

Hybrid Topology

It is a combined topology. Hybrid topology is a bit easy to understand because if more than one topology is added then it becomes a Hybrid topology. If two different things are combined, it becomes a Hybrid that we know.

EX-Suppose state bank is using bus topology on one branch and ring topology is being used on state bank's other bench, if state bank joins these two branches then it will become Hybrid topology.

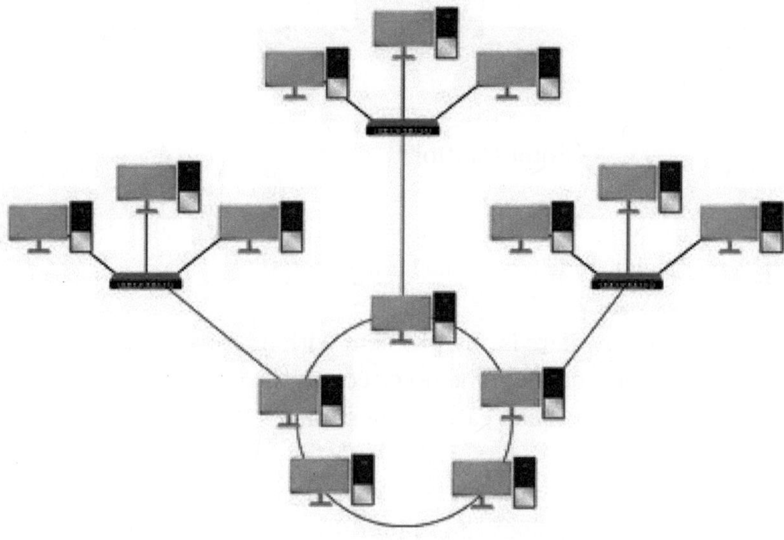

Enter Caption

Advantage of Hybrid Topology

- It is very secure and reliable.
- You can establish this topology according to your requirement.
- If a device is added or removed in this topology, then there will be no effect on the entire network.
- You can take advantage of the topology you will use within this topology.
- You can expand this topology as much as you want.

Disadvantage of Hybrid Topology

1. A lot of cable wire is needed to establish this topology.
2. Its major disadvantage is that the design of this topology is very complicated.
3. If any problem comes in this topology, it is a bit difficult to solve it.

Tree Topology

It is based on a tree structure. There is only one difference between tree topology and hybrid topology. In hybrid topology, you can use any topology, but in tree topology, bus topology and star topology are made together.

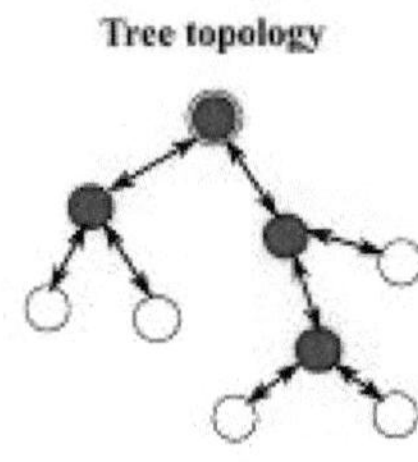

Enter Caption

Advantage of Tree Topology

- It is a very fast topology. Finding a particular node is very fast and easy.
- You can expand this topology as much as you want.
- You can easily understand this topology and if there is any problem with it, you can easily solve it.
- If the connecting cable breaks for any reason, there will be no effect on the entire network.
- The design of this topology is a bit simple and you can easily understand.

Disadvantage of Tree Topology

1. Many different devices are required in this topology, so it is a bit costly to implement this topology.
2. If there is a problem in any device inside this topology, it is a bit difficult to troubleshoot it.
3. In this topology, if the backbone cable of the tree topology breaks down, then the network of the entire tree topology will not be affected.
4. If a device is added to this topology, then configuring that device is a bit difficult

12.6 Types of Network

There are many types of computer networks. They have been divided according to their size, geographic area. Starting from a small room, a network can connect computers from all over the world. So let's know the Types of Networks.

Basically, there are three types of networks LAN, MAN, and WAN.

LAN (Local Area Network)

Local Area Network means LAN. You will find this network everywhere like banks, offices, colleges, schools, business organizations. This network is used for resource sharing, data storage, document printing. To make this, not much hardware is required, just a hub, switch, network adapter, router, and Ethernet cable are needed.

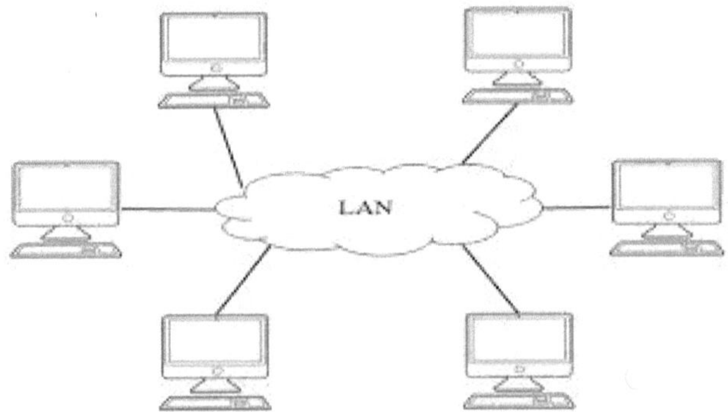

The smallest LAN can be made of only two computers. We can connect nearly 1000 computers in a LAN. Mostly LAN is used in wire connections. But nowadays it is also being used in wireless. The main characteristics of this network are its speed, low cost, and security. Ethernet cable is used to set up LAN.

This network is special for document sharing and printing in an office. What happens in document sharing? There is a central server where all the files are kept. Which any employee can access the file without going there. If someone also wants to print, he can print using the central printer. This is the advantage of LAN. This is called resource sharing.

If a local area network is wireless then it is called wireless LAN.

Advantage

Used in a home, office, and college.

Its distance is limited in the small geographical area

This network can be created easily

The data transmission speed of this network is very high

MAN (Metropolitan Area Network)

This is a network connecting an entire city. This network connects all the small and big colleges, schools, government offices, banks in a city. MAN is a bigger network than LAN. MAN covers from 10KM up to 100KM. It is used to make a big network by connecting many LANs together.

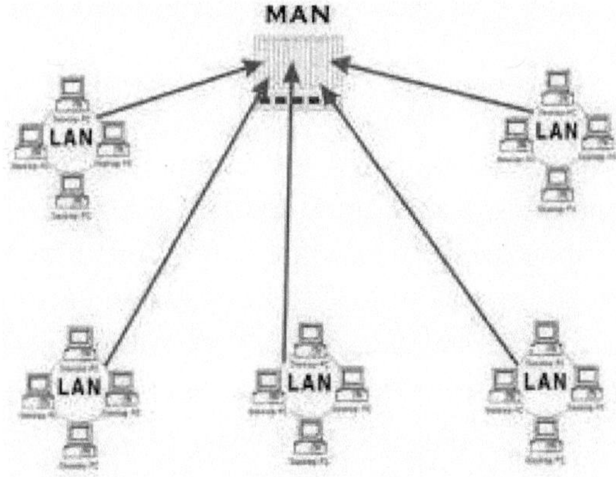

Enter Caption

If such networks are used in a college campus, then it is called a campus area network. The best example of this is the cable TV network. MAN is used to connect LAN to LAN. Any big business organization becomes its own MAN. Through which he can connect his different branches.

Advantage

It covers more area.

Its distance is limited in a large geographical area like towns, cities.

Its ownership is public and private.

Installing this network costs more than LAN.

The data transmission speed is moderate.

WAN (Wide Area Network)

This is the largest network that keeps computers from all over the world connected. It is also called WAN. A wide area network is called LAN of LANs. The specialty of this network is that it has a low DATA rate, but covers more distance. The best example of a Wide Area Network is the Internet.

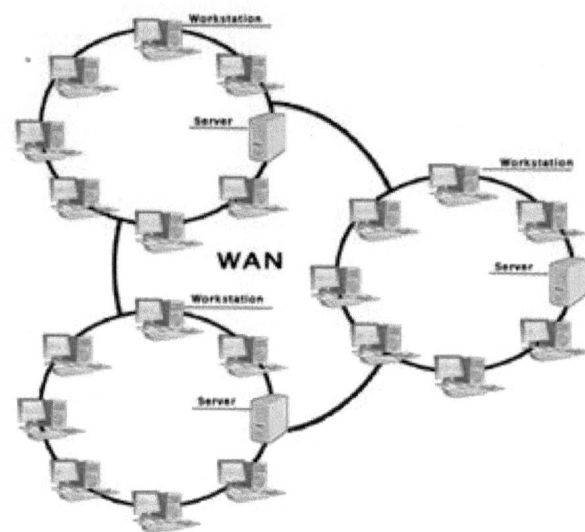

There are two types of WAN Enterprise WAN and Global WAN. Computers connected to a wide area network mostly use public networks such as telephone lines, leased lines, and satellites. The largest WAN is the Internet. There are many Wide Area Networks. Like public packet networks, Large Corporate networks, Military networks, banking networks, Railway reservation networks and finally Airline Reservation networks.

The company providing network facilities through WAN is called Network Service Provider. They are called the core of the Internet. WAN is said to be the most expensive network because some such technology is used in it such as SONET, Frame Relay, and ATM.

Advantage

It can cover a very large area. And with its help computers from all over the world can be connected.

A large geographical area like two countries can connect with this network

Its ownership is public and private

This network is complicated to install and maintain

12.7 Internet

Internet is a network of many different types of networks.

The Internet is actually a global wide area network that connects computer systems around the world. It consists of many high-bandwidth data lines which are called the "backbone" of the Internet. These lines are connected with major Internet hubs that distribute data to other locations, such as web servers and ISPs. Whereas, if you want to connect to the Internet, and then you must have access to an Internet service provider (ISP), which acts as a mediator between you and the Internet. Most ISPs provide broadband Internet access via a cable, DSL, or fiber connection. When you connect to the Internet via a public Wi-Fi signal, the Wi-Fi router is also connected to an ISP to provide you with the Internet.

Nowadays internet can also be used with the help of mobile phone where in cellular data towers also have to be connected to one or the other Internet service provider to provide internet access to the connected devices.

Features of the Internet

Let us now know about the features of the Internet, which are very important to know.

WWW (World Wide Web)

Content that runs over the internet is called web. www is a system that is used to access the web server. (A server is an integrated place where all content of a particular company or organization is stored.) The World Wide Web is a part of the Internet, which supports hypertext documents, while it allows users to view and navigate different types of data. Whereas a web page is a document that is encoded with hypertext markup language (HTML) tags.

HTML allows designers to be linked together via hyperlinks. Every web page has an address, which is called a uniform resource locator (URL). Using URL you can access a particular server.

E-mail

With the help of e-mail, we can send any message to anyone in any corner of the world in a very short time with security. Electronic mail (e-mail) is a very popular reason due to which people use the internet. To create, send, and receive e-mail messages, you need an e-mail program and an account in an Internet mail server with a domain name. To use e-mail, it is very important for a user to have an e-mail address, which you can create by adding your username to e-mail. For example, if you want to create your account in Gmail, then you can create like username@gmail.com. Here you have to choose a slightly unique username that is not already available in a particular organization. Mostly nowadays many companies like Gmail yahoo Rediff mails provide this service for free.

FTP (File transfer protocol)

FTP is used to transfer a file from one location to another location on the internet. Basically, it is used to send files from server to client. Client means a user of the internet. It is an internet tool used to copy files from one computer to another. Using a special FTP program or a web browser, you can log in to an ETP host computer, over the Internet and copy files to your computer.FTP is very handy to find and copy software files, while you can do the same with articles and other types of data types. Universities and software companies use FTP servers so that they can allow visitors to access data.

Telnet

Telnet is used to access any device remotely. Telnet is a specialized service that allows you to access the contents of another computer using a computer with the help of a telnet host. Creates a telnet program on a "Window" host so that you can access files, issue commands, and exchange data. Telnet is widely used by libraries so that it allows visitors to view information, find articles, etc.

IRC (Internet Relay Chat)

Internet Relay Chat (IRC) is a service that allows users to communicate with each other in real-time by typing text in a special window. Just like the news, there are hundreds of IRC "channels" and each one is dedicated to a single subject or user group. If you wish, you can use a special IRC program to participate in these chat room discussions, but most chat rooms are set up on the website itself, which enables visitors directly from their browser window to chat.

12.8 Internet Intranet and Extranet

Intranet

Intranet is a sub domain of the internet. It is a kind of private network. It is used in a company, college institution, bank which is also called Local Area Network. It is a completely secure network. Valid Username and Password are required to access Intranet. It is a network used as the Internet. But to use it, the user must have a user ID. It cannot be used without a user ID. So there is no risk of it being hacked. In this, some computers are connected with each other. And the exchange of data is also possible between them.

Advantage of Intranet

Through this comes an improvement in communication. Managers can share their team's ideas well and managers and employees can communicate clearly. This also improves productivity. The company's intranet can also give access to all the tools and information to the employees. Staff members can increase their productivity by doing more and more tasks in the intranet itself. Many companies use it to organize and automate their work process.

Extranet

An extranet is a common network of internet and intranet. It is a part of the intranet itself. When someone accesses the intranet through the Internet, the system to access this is called an extranet. It is a communication network that is based on (TCP/IP). Simply put, when a person uses the Internet and wants to provide his information outside his network area, then he has to exchange data through the Internet by seeing a user ID and password to the outsider.

Advantage of Extranet

There are also some main advantages of using Extranet, we will know this further. It acts as a medium between the company and the business partners. If customers have any complaints or queries, a platform is provided to resolve them.

Internet

Intranet

Extranet

In general it can be accessed without user name or password.

Only with valid Username and Password it is accessed Intranet.

Username and Password are required to access this too.

Internet can be accessed and managed by any one or any organization

Only authorized users and particular organization can access or managed intranet.

Extranet can be accessed and managed by more than one organization.

Its security depends on the user's device. And it is less secure.

Its security depends on the firewall. And it is highly secure.

Its security is dependent on the firewall of the Internet, Extranet. It is comparatively less secure then Intranet and higher then internet

It is an example of public network.

It is an example of private network.

It is an example of both public and private network that provides data with the help of a public network.

The following diagram illustrates the differences between the internet, intranet, and extranet.

Extranet

Intranet

Internet

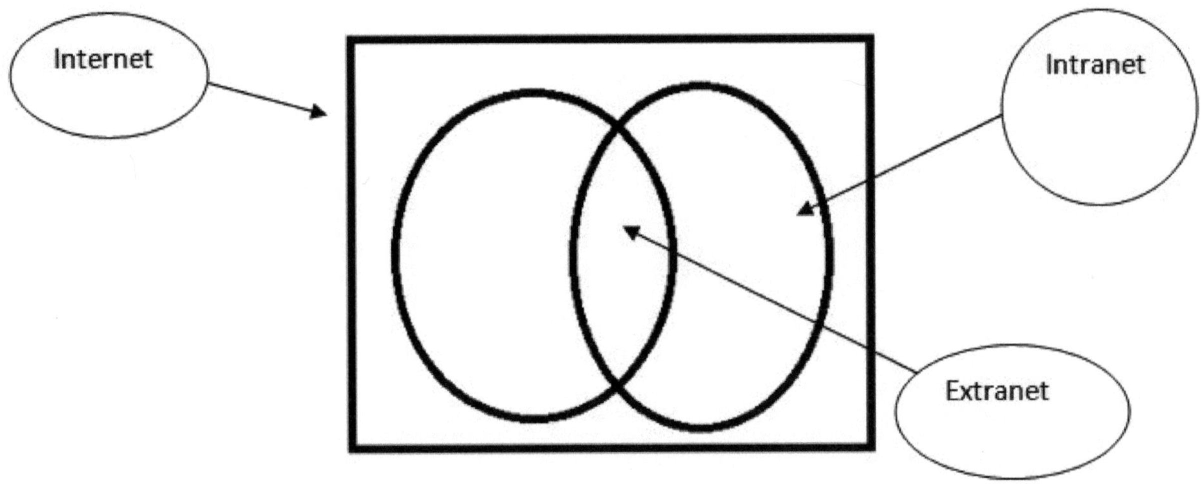

Exercises

Objective type question

Choose the correct answer for the followings

1.________________ is the technology that connects the computers within a small area.

(a)LAN (b) MAN (c) WAN (d) PAN

2. A computer network permits sharing of

(a)Data (b) information (c) resources (d) all of these

3. A _____ is a standard set of rules that determines how computers communicate with each other across networks.

(a)Protomol (b) Protochol (c) Protocool (d) Protocol

4. The advantage of a LAN is

(a)Saving all your data (b) Accessing the web (c) Backing up your data (d) sharing peripherals

5. Communication between a computer and a keyboard involves ________________transmission

(a) Full-duplex (b) Half-duplex (c) Simplex (d) None of these

6. Which topology requires a central controller or hub?

(a) Star (b) Mesh (c) Bus (d) Ring

7. The information to be communicated in a data communications system is the _________

(a) Medium (b) Protocol (c) Transmission (d) Message

8. In ________ transmission, the channel capacity is shared by both communicating devices at all times.

(a)Full-duplex (b) Simplex (c) Half-duplex (d) Half-Simplex

9. Which topology requires a multipoint connection?

(a) Mesh (b) Star (c) Ring (d) Bus

10. A cable break in a ________ topology stops all transmission.

(a) Mesh (b) Star (c) Ring (d) Bus

Theoretical questions

1. What do you mean by LAN? Explain the suitable topologies of local area networking.
2. What is data communication? Describe its elements and media.
3. Distinguish between LAN, MAN, and WAN.
4. Describe different topologies with the help of a diagram.
5. Differentiate between wired and wireless data communication with the help of an example.
6. Explain in detail various guided media of data transmission.
7. Write in detail about simplex, half-duplex, and full-duplex transmission mode.
8. List and explain different networking devices. Also, give the reason for using such devices.
9. Define and explain internet, intranet, and extranet.

Printed by Libri Plureos GmbH in Hamburg,
Germany